Proust's
Macaroon

Proust's Macaroon

James Wood

PICULET PRESS
NEW YORK
2010

Piculet Press books can be ordered from online booksellers
or through bookstores.
Amazon.com handles all Piculet books.

CATALOGING DATA

Wood, James.
Proust's macaroon / by James Wood. – 1st ed.

ISBN 978-0-9825753-0-7

1. Legal profession—Drama. 2. Legal ethics—Drama.
3. Lawyers in love—Drama. 4. Legal education—Drama.
5. Work—Drama. 6. Tragicomedy.

Library of Congress Control Number 2010924383

Book design and composition by John Balkwill
Lumino Press · Santa Barbara
Cover design by Sybille Schenker
Cover photograph by Max Klimt

CHARACTERS

JOHN BOTZ: an associate in the law firm of
Biggins, Tostick & Thomas, LLP

ELLEN MILLER: an associate

BRAD THOMAS: the Managing Partner

CHARLIE HOWARD: the Administrator of the firm

ERNIE TUMMEL: a former associate

GIORGIO: a pet rat

SPEEDBALL: a pigeon

Proust's
Macaroon

Act One

Scene One

Thursday morning in the supply loft of Biggins, Tostick & Thomas, LLP, a law firm. The space is nondescript, furnished with institutional furniture: a desk; a long table or two; a dilapidated sofa covered with file folders. One table has large cardboard boxes on it and under it. Beyond these items, simply a computer, some chairs and the usual paraphernalia of a supply/storage room—filing cabinets, some shelves for books, files, etc. An open door in the upstage wall and a door in each side wall would be useful.

Voices are heard offstage and two sets of approaching footsteps, one normal, the other marked by the sound of a cane striking the floor.

CHARLIE
Good to have you back, John. Good to have you back.

JOHN
Charlie, slow down. What's going on? I want to go to my office.

CHARLIE
I know, I know.

CHARLIE enters wearing a dress shirt, bow tie, Bermuda shorts held up by suspenders, high sox and running shoes.

Voilà! Here we are. Chick, chickee boom chickee.

JOHN limps in behind CHARLIE wearing a suit, tie and baseball cap. He has a full length walking cast on one leg and is using a cane.

JOHN
So what are we doing in the fucking supply loft?

CHARLIE
You've been out. A lot's happened. . . . How does it look?

JOHN
Better, better than I remember. Dominoes. Certain other memories.

CHARLIE
Missed my old domino partner. . . . Did some rearranging, made it neater, more comfortable.

JOHN
Charlie, I should talk to Murray.

CHARLIE
Dragged the desk out, dusted it off.

JOHN
I should talk to Murray right away.

CHARLIE
Try it.

JOHN
Try what?

CHARLIE
The desk.

JOHN
What for?

CHARLIE
(Pulling out the chair) C'mon, humor me. Sit.

JOHN
Then I gotta report to Murray, get back in the swing, do some work. (Moving around behind the desk and sitting) Very nice, Charlie, very nice.

CHARLIE

Talked to anyone?

JOHN

Just in from the boonies, remember?

CHARLIE

Ellen?

JOHN

Quick call to make a date. She's in D.C.

CHARLIE

She's back. Hasn't told you anything?

JOHN

About what?

CHARLIE

You know, the firm, B,T&T?

JOHN

With Ellen business and personal never meet.

CHARLIE

Well, we all have our rules.

JOHN

Look, Charlie, I want to see Murray.

CHARLIE

Sit. Sit still a minute. . . . Murray's gone, John.

JOHN

Gone?

CHARLIE

Defected, switched law firms.

JOHN

What the fuck you talking about?

CHARLIE

Files, furniture, went out on the weekend. Hasn't been around since Tuesday.

JOHN

Left the firm?

CHARLIE

Partner at Gladwell, Heifitz & Harriman now.

JOHN

Left Biggins, Tostick & Thomas?

CHARLIE

Took his clients . . . and none of his associates. *(Taking an envelope from his pocket)* For you.

JOHN

(Opening the envelope and reading the letter) Jesus. And I killed myself for that dude.

CHARLIE

Alas, collegiality hath its limits.

JOHN

Splits and leaves me with the offer of a reference. I thought I worked here.

CHARLIE

There's more. *(Pause)* He wanted to fire you, in absentia.

JOHN

Murray?

CHARLIE

Brad.

JOHN

What for?

CHARLIE

While you were in hospital.

JOHN

For getting hurt?

CHARLIE

For falling off the billing truck. *(Pause)* With Murray gone, who's
going to feed you work, John? *(Silence)* Going to fire you, he was.
Not good, I thought. Lose my domino partner. "Illegal, Brad," I
told him. "Firing a man who's out with a broken peg will create big
liabilities, cost you money." Made it all up, of course. Boom chickee
boom. But he bought it.

JOHN

Thanks, Charlie.

CHARLIE

Couldn't save your office, though.

JOHN

What?

CHARLIE

You are now seated at your new desk.

JOHN

The supply loft my office? Charlie! Tell me you're kidding!

CHARLIE

"Put him up in the supply loft, Charlie. See how that gilded little
fart likes it up there away from his deep pile carpet, high tech furniture. Can't hurt the firm's business, hasn't got any clients to meet
now anyway."

JOHN

Jesus.

CHARLIE

That's our Managing Partner. He'll be up to see you, John. To gloat, if nothing worse.

JOHN

Some office.

CHARLIE

You just said you always liked it up here.

JOHN

You know what the fuck I mean, Charlie.

CHARLIE

Look. Look John, try looking at it this way. Think of this place as sanctuary, cozy sanctuary atop the frantic, opulent, materialistic law firm below.

JOHN

Right, sure.

CHARLIE

Floating serenely over the treadmill, the decadence . . .

JOHN

Charlie! My office is down there, down there! My opulent office. I belong in that decadence. Why do you think I took the bar?

CHARLIE

Released, cut loose from the throbbing, pulsing, thrusting organism. Serene . . .

JOHN

I'm an associate. Who ever heard of a serene associate?

CHARLIE

Freed from that forcing house of adversarial bacteria. *(Pause)* A place for the wounded warrior to recover. . . .

JOHN

Is it over? Have you finished?

CHARLIE

Boom chickee . . . chickee . . . Yeah.

JOHN

Well, screw 'em, Charlie. I'm going to survive. Here! At Biggins, Tostick & Thomas!

CHARLIE

You're a good lawyer, John.

JOHN

Three months more and I'm out of the probationary period.

CHARLIE

We all got our goals. . . .

JOHN

Then if they fire me, at least I get severance.

CHARLIE

Me, I've got six months to retirement and my pension. Assuming they have enough current income to pay it.

JOHN

I've worked too goddamn hard.

CHARLIE

Nothing's funded.

JOHN

And the money. Let's be honest, I need the money.

CHARLIE

Murray's gone, John.

JOHN

But I didn't come here just for money, let alone for severance, I came to stay. Some day I want to make partner. I want to belong, be a permanent part of this firm, of the family.

CHARLIE

Families break up, John, even real ones.

JOHN

A partner here, at B,T&T.

CHARLIE

Murray, your mentor and protector, is gone.

JOHN

I will, you watch, Charlie. By God, I will.

CHARLIE

Who's going to feed you work?

JOHN

(Long pause) Yeah, in the end, after all the brave talk, what the hell am I going to do? (Silence) Charlie?

CHARLIE

You know me. I play dominoes, shoot the shit. But I'm not the firm therapist.

JOHN

You must have a suggestion.

CHARLIE

And I don't give advice. . . . So what was it like in the hospital?

JOHN

Boring. Also scary.

CHARLIE

Always hated 'em.

JOHN

Six guys in the ward and two die.

CHARLIE

Skiing's gotten more dangerous than I realized.

JOHN

These were townies, old guy fell off his roof trying to fix a leak. . . .
And this kid, Tom, in the bed next to mine, who'd laid his Yamaha
down on some ice.

CHARLIE

Ugh, old guys one thing, young folks another. We only get one ride,
John. Pay attention.

JOHN

Yeah, I know. Lying there, many black thoughts, doubts. (*Pause*)
But now I'm back, ready to go. If I can find some goddamn work.
Never had this problem before, always the opposite with Murray.

CHARLIE

Yeah, Murray's a tiger. Was, that is.

JOHN

(*Looking around*) This place still double as your city pigeon coop?

CHARLIE

That is true, the case.

JOHN

Am I sharing with anyone?

CHARLIE

Just Speedball.

JOHN

Ahh, now I catch the faint aroma. Where is he?

CHARLIE

She. Behind that filing cabinet which, incidentally, now contains your files. *(Holding up* SPEEDBALL's *cage)* You hear anyone coming, keep her out of sight. And one of the boxes here, under the table, that's more stuff from your old office, pictures, things in your desk, some books. Well, I gotta go.

JOHN

Charlie, wait. Wait a minute.

CHARLIE

Yeah?

JOHN

Look, you are the firm's Administrator and, . . .

CHARLIE

(Interrupting) And I can't help you.

JOHN

But you're supposed to assign work to associates, theoretically at least.

CHARLIE

Theory's fine but we live in detail. Fact is I've got nothing to assign, John, nothing.

JOHN

(In general) Goddamn it!

CHARLIE

C'mon, you're young, you'll survive . . . somewhere.

JOHN

Nothing?

CHARLIE

Nothing. Even if I wanted to break my rules, get involved.

JOHN

Jesus, don't get involved.

CHARLIE

Look, John, you any idea how many young attorneys I've seen go through this turnstile over the years? Scores, seems like hundreds. Visions of lemmings. What if I'd tried to help each one? And what could I have done if I tried? If you can't help, keep your distance, I say. . . . OK, yeah, perfect. Case in point. (*Lifting boxes from the floor to the table*) Take this stuff. What in the hell could I have done for him?

JOHN

Who?

CHARLIE

Ernie Tummel here. I've got to sort through this stuff and ship it off to him. His sister's been calling me, says he's ranting, not taking his medication. I don't want him showing up here.

JOHN

Tummel?

CHARLIE

Been gone some time.

JOHN

I've gone from the bone-ward to the bone-yard.

CHARLIE

Ernie was definitely a casualty. Made the Faustian bargain: Bartered his soul for The Law.

JOHN

Casualty?

CHARLIE

Bright guy, law review, clerk for judge on an appeals court. Been on
Brad's team for some time so he was stressed out anyway. Then one
day Brad has him depose this disturbed woman, a debtor, here in
the office. Brad knew she was suicidal but didn't tell Ernie. Dumb
case anyway, favor for a wealthy client. Woman was an honest pau-
per, no assets, no lawyer. Ernie pressed too hard and suddenly she
starts screaming, opens her handbag, whips out a vial . . .

JOHN

(Interrupting) Wait! Whips out what?

CHARLIE

A vial, v-i-a-l—Don't you ever read detective novels, mysteries,
thrillers? Vial full of red liquid. She starts screaming suicide, "You're
killing me! Murderer!" she yells. Then she shakes the vial. Fluid
begins to bubble and froth and run all over her dress and shoes. She
puts vial to her lips and gulps it down, residue dribbling down her
bosom. Then she collapses, falls to the floor a sodden, red-stained
heap. Court reporter faints.

JOHN

She die?

CHARLIE

Court reporter?

JOHN

No, the . . . ahh, vial lady.

CHARLIE

She did not. Vial fluid was cranberry juice and soda water. But there
were cops and ambulances and hospitalization and tabloid attention. So Brad fired Ernie. Few days later, Ernie went bonkers in
a major way. (Pause) All I could do for him was dump his stuff in
these boxes and store it till he got better.

JOHN

What's he doing now?

CHARLIE

Sick a long time. Marriage broke up. Wife moved across the country with the kids. He's doing leg work for some insurance adjuster, I think. Lives in a small town in the northern part of the state. Huntersfield? Yeah, Huntersfield.

JOHN

Jesus, the bush . . .

CHARLIE

Some people call it the country.

JOHN

Charlie, I've seen the place. It's nowhere, especially for someone like Ernie. Came to the big city full of hope, had a taste of the dream. Now he's lost in the stars, banished to one of those tiny rectangles of orange lights you see in the night from the Red-Eye. Everything floating in a black sea of loneliness . . . abandoned mill, market, liquor store, couple of gas stations, a few bars, church or two, and a building that'll be mustard-colored in the morning with a Loyal Order of Moose sign swinging from the second story. It's not the country, it's a kind of death, the associate's nightmare: slouching back to Huntersfield to do contract work.

CHARLIE

Very poetic. I like it but could get you into trouble.

JOHN

Trouble is where I am now, Charlie.

CHARLIE

You and all the others, past and present, have my sympathy. What the hell, I was an associate once myself. But I can't save you.

JOHN

I just want some leads, Charlie. You know, partners who might need temporary help on a project, unfinished stuff that's lying around, junk work no one wants. You must have some ideas. Whatever you say, you are The Grand Administrator.

CHARLIE
I wish you'd stop calling me that. Means nothing. You know partners get the business and dole out the work themselves.

JOHN
What about *Il Duce*? He must have a lot of stuff.

CHARLIE
I'd forget that appellation, if I were you.

JOHN
You're giving advice, Charlie.

CHARLIE
So make the most of it. Don't expect Brad to save you unless he's desperate. *(Pause)* Well, I'm going. See, I copped your old computer for you. No phone line yet but I'm working on it.

JOHN
No phone! Come on, Charlie, how the hell am I supposed to be a lawyer here if I'm not on the firm's switchboard?

CHARLIE
Hey, you're lucky to be in the house. Boom chickee boom. Meantime, pound on the floor if you get desperate. My office is right under here, remember?

JOHN
Despite the look of it, my head's fine. I remember everything . . . except the accident. (CHARLIE *begins to leave.*) Hey, Charlie, it's Thursday. We on for dominoes tonight?

CHARLIE
You remembered. Yeah, OK, sure. See you tonight. Au revoir.

CHARLIE *exits.*

(JOHN *sits a moment, turns his cap around visor-backwards and limps over to talk to* SPEEDBALL *behind the filing cabinet.*)

Scene Two

JOHN

Ah, *mi piccione bello.*

ELLEN *enters unnoticed by* JOHN.

ELLEN

Ahem!

JOHN

(Bouncing up from behind the file cabinet) Ehhh, . . . Ellie! . . .
Wow! . . . You look fantastic! Long time, such a long time.

ELLEN

Yeah. Well, you should cool the Italian chit-chat. What if I'd been
our Managing Partner?

JOHN

I'd have said, "*Pace, Il Duce, pace.*"

ELLEN

Jesus, they really have put you in with the birds. Pigeons! In a law
firm.

JOHN

Happens all the time, staple of a lawyer's diet. *(Taking off the cloth
that covers* SPEEDBALL's *cage)* Meet Speedball.

ELLEN

He looks stupid, totally.

JOHN

She.

ELLEN

What?

JOHN

Ellie, Speedball is a lady. (*Pause*) Ellie, Ellie. Let me look at you. Seems like years.

ELLEN

You don't look so bad, yourself, considering. But what's with the hat? You got a skateboard too? (*As she approaches,* JOHN *starts to embrace her.*)

You out of your mind? Himself could walk in here any minute. Just want to inspect the damages.

(*She lifts his hat as he bends down toward her and we see the reddish, lacerated top of his head. She looks without expression, replaces the hat and turns away.*)

Well, I see why you wear the hat.

JOHN

Ellie, let me look at you.

ELLEN

(*Warming a little*) You keep saying that. So look. But make it fast. I can only stay a minute.

JOHN

You do look fantastic.

ELLEN

I don't usually look so hot?

JOHN

You were always, you are, uniformly gorgeous . . . but, Ellie, those rags . . .

ELLEN

Power lunch today.

JOHN

Who's the lucky . . .

ELLEN

(*Interrupting*) We're still on for tomorrow night? . . .

JOHN

Absolutely.

ELLEN

Haven't seen you for a long time, John. (*Pause*) Lots has happened.

JOHN

Charlie told me.

ELLEN

Charlie! Now there's a suicidal role model for you. Bermuda shorts, babbling French.

JOHN

Hey, I like Charlie. He's highly intelligent. He . . .

ELLEN

(*Interrupting*) Brilliant law school record, promising young associate, budding anti-trust wizard. Good old "chickee chickee boom chickee." Can't believe they've kept him around. Must know where the bodies are buried.

JOHN

He's the only one who can find anything. Besides, he understands computers, networking . . .

ELLEN

Networks.

JOHN

What?

ELLEN

Women do networking. Men do networks.

JOHN

Oh.

ELLEN

The first's humane, the other's just hardwiring. . . . God, I'm really bitchy. Johnny, I'm sorry. . . . You probably wish you'd never met me.

JOHN

I'm not complaining.

ELLEN

I'm really sorry.

JOHN

For what?

ELLEN

Everything. The accident . . . Murray . . . You losing your office. Especially the accident. (*Pause*) And I felt awful leaving you like that.

JOHN

You had to get back.

ELLEN

You wouldn't have . . . If it'd been me, you'd have stayed. Or, you'd have gone back to visit me. Wouldn't you? Called, emailed, texted, whatever, more often. You would, I'm sure of it.

JOHN

Who knows, Ellie, who knows?

ELLEN

Christ, I'm so sorry.

JOHN

Ellie, it's OK.

ELLEN

And I still haven't sent the CDs I promised to Tom and Mary. Bought 'em but got busy . . .

JOHN

Tom died, Ellie.

ELLEN

Jesus! They were just going to fix his leg?

JOHN

Anesthetic killed him.

ELLEN

God, he was so young and . . . beautiful. They both were so beautiful. Now, I feel really guilty.

JOHN

You could still send them to Mary. I know she'd like to hear from you.

ELLEN

Yeah, maybe I'll do that. Don't know what I'd say though, not sure she'd want them now. Music brings things back. *(Pause)* As soon as I started to leave you I wanted to go back. But when I got here, Brad gave me this, this humongous job.

JOHN

Big deal?

ELLEN

You could say that.

JOHN

Want to tell me about it?

ELLEN

Cut, cut, cut! You know the rules. Let's just say it looks like the big test.

JOHN

You make the A-team! Partnership!

ELLEN

Junior, modified, entry level, whatever . . . but, yeah, I have reason to believe . . . For godsake don't say anything. I could be wrong.

JOHN

Ellie, that's wonderful!

ELLEN

Not yet. And if I fuck up, I won't get another chance. Not the way things are around here.

JOHN

Tell me about it!

ELLEN

Yeah, I don't have to tell you. Sorry I didn't tip you about Murray when we talked. Didn't think of it till I'd hung up. Preoccupied, I guess. SO tired! Washington was awful. *(Pause)* Still want to do tomorrow night, huh?

JOHN

Sure. Eyetalian cuisine at my dump, some delicious fish, a little video perhaps, the night, the whole damn weekend, in fact. But maybe we should go out, celebrate? You want to do something tonight?

ELLEN

God no. I'm dead.

JOHN

(Pause) Your voice. Love your voice.

ELLEN

You do?

JOHN

Really missed it. Smoky, musical. (ELLEN *chuckles.*) Your laugh too. Reminds me of a good trout stream.

ELLEN

C'mon, you got fish on the brain. What brought this on?

JOHN

What can I say? Love. *(Pause)* Love.

ELLEN

(Smiling) Forget the bullshit. . . . Brad said anything to you?

JOHN

Aggravated by separation, addiction.

ELLEN

C'mon, answer the question.

JOHN

Ughh, the law's making you hard. Naw, haven't seen Brad.

ELLEN

Well, I unhh . . . I overheard something.

JOHN

Overheard what?

ELLEN

Umm, Maxine, Maxine saying Brad's been talking about you.

JOHN

Yeah?

ELLEN

So what are you doing to drum up some work?

JOHN

Hey, ease up. I just got here.

ELLEN

With no Murray how are you going to bill a lousy ten minutes, let alone hour, for chrissake?

JOHN

Besides, you said, 'Cut, cut, cut.' That only cut one way?

ELLEN

Just trying to help, that's all. Know this place better than you do, working here longer.

JOHN

You want to help? Get me some work. What about the thing you're working on? (*Silence*) Research, something. Break your rule for your favorite broken leg?

ELLEN

(ELLEN's *cell phone rings.*) Hello . . . Hello. . . . Jesus, lost it! They're after me. Lemme use your phone.

JOHN

Sorry, don't have one yet.

ELLEN

Banished to the boonies and no wire: you are in trouble! (*Going out a side door*) Well, remember, be careful if you see Brad. He sounded really nasty, . . . unnh, so Maxine said. (*Pause*) I'll stop by before I go home. And hide that pigeon house.

ELLEN *exits.*

SCENE THREE

JOHN *sits quietly a few moments then, hearing a heavy tread off-stage, he leaves his cane at his desk and limps over to hide* SPEED-BALL's *cage behind the filing cabinet.*

BRAD *enters.*

BRAD

Anybody home? I see the stick, but where's the gimp? (*Noises behind the filing cabinet, then* JOHN *emerges, cap turned back visor-first.*) Hi, John Boy. Whatcha been doing back there?

JOHN

Brad! I, uh . . . nothing.

BRAD

"Nuthin?" Doin "nuthin," John Boy? So we got plenty of nuthin. Haw, haw.

JOHN

(*Quietly aside*) Musical comedy, already?

BRAD

How's that?

JOHN

What?

BRAD

I was saying and you interrupted me.

JOHN

Sorry.

BRAD

Sounded like "enemy." You think I'm the enemy?

JOHN

No, no. Of course, not.

BRAD

(*Suddenly genial*) So, how's everything?

JOHN

OK.

BRAD

Shit, this place is Outer Siberia, the Globi Desert. Had a hell of a
time finding you.

JOHN

Yeah, I bet.

BRAD

So why has he done this?

JOHN

Huh?

BRAD

Why has he put you up here? What happened to your old office?
Couldn't he find anything better than this?

JOHN

Who?

BRAD

Charlie. Charlie Howard. Our famous, all-powerful Administrator.
How could he put you up here?

JOHN

Unhh . . .

BRAD

But, aside from this dump, everything's OK?

JOHN
Fine. You know, still in a cast, still using a cane, . . . but, yeah, fine.

BRAD
Canes, oh yeah. The mother had one of those. In a wheelchair now.

JOHN
Sorry to hear that, Brad.

BRAD
Naw, much better. Easier to keep track of her. Stairs stop her, and so on. . . . Broke the ole hip, huh?

JOHN
Leg.

BRAD
Real good, huh?

JOHN
What's that?

BRAD
Hear it was serious.

JOHN
(Pointing to his lower leg) Yeah, both bones, down below the. . .

BRAD
Missed a lot of work, huh?

JOHN
What? No, no, only a couple of weeks. And now I'm back.

BRAD
What's with the baseball cap? New uniform for associates?

JOHN
Yeah, no. Had some lacerations, stitches. Thought a fedora or a

watch cap would look worse. *(Starting to take off his hat)* Want to see my war wounds?

> BRAD

Aggh, no, no, for God's sake. Keep the fucking hat on. Thanks all the same. . . . Well, well, well. That's what you get for going skiing with a pro. You shouldda hung out in the bar back at the lodge and let her rule the slopes. Haw, haw. Know what I mean.

> JOHN

When we go skiing, I ski alone. I was hurt in a car accident, Brad. Thought you knew that.

> BRAD

Oh, yeah. I forget. Ellie's a great skier but shitty driver, right?

> JOHN

I didn't say that.

> BRAD

Naw. I say that. Insurance company does too.

> JOHN

I don't remember the accident at all.

> BRAD

Well, she's scared the hell out of me too.

> JOHN

You've been driving with Ellen?

> BRAD

Oh, you know, on our way to court and stuff. Very aggressive behind the wheel. Know what I mean. And at the Bar. Clients love her.

> JOHN

I bet.

                    BRAD
The best. But you getting along all right?

                    JOHN
What?

                    BRAD
Here, I mean?

                    JOHN
Well, sure, all right.

                    BRAD
Have everything you need?

                    JOHN
Well, yeah, almost. Almost everything.

                    BRAD
Everybody treating you OK?

                    JOHN
What?

                    BRAD
Finding your way around?

                    JOHN
Brad, I've been here a long time now.

                    BRAD
Right, and I don't get it. A fuckin full-rate mystery . . .

                    JOHN
What is?

                    BRAD
You. You unhappy here?

JOHN

No!

BRAD

Haven't I treated you OK?

JOHN

Sure, I mean, you know, I was working mostly for Murray and all but, sure.

BRAD

(Silence) You heard about Murray.

JOHN

Oh, yeah. Charlie told me and . . . (Gesturing around the space)

BRAD

Of course. Real stupid of me. Sure, you'd have heard about that. . . . But you agree the firm's treated you right?

JOHN

Yes.

BRAD

Fairly. Pay OK? Given you a chance?

JOHN

Yes, and I've tried to make the most of it.

BRAD

Yeah?

JOHN

I've worked hard, Brad. You can ask Murray . . . well . . .

BRAD

Very funny. . . . Listen, John Boy, if your work for Murray was that hot, how come he didn't take you with him when he bugged out?

JOHN

He didn't take anybody, Brad. You know that.

BRAD

I know that and I don't see why we should keep what he didn't
want. Know what I mean.

JOHN

He said Gladwell wouldn't let him bring anybody.

BRAD

"He said!" So! You talked it all over with him! Now we're beginning
to get the fucking picture. You knew all this was going to happen and
didn't say one goddamn word. Maybe that's why you went skiing.

JOHN

No, Brad, no. He didn't tell me, not before he left the firm, not ever.
He wrote to me, while I was gone. (*Waving letter*) Wrote to all of
us, I guess. After. Charlie just gave it to me.

BRAD

Wait a minute. You said, "he said."

JOHN

Slip of the tongue, Brad. That's all.

BRAD

Slip of the tongue, eh?

JOHN

I haven't talked to him, Brad.

BRAD

The witness changes his story.

JOHN

No Brad, I promise you.

BRAD

Well, I've been doing some figuring. What can we do with John Boy now that Daddy's gone? Very discouraging. Know what I mean.

JOHN

Discouraging?

BRAD

Worse. Terminal. You just got in with the wrong fella. Murray hired you and now he's bugged out, stolen a bunch of our clients, left you dangling in the wind. And you got no clients of your own. What can I say? (*Pause*) You take a long weekend and vanish. Then you come back here with a baseball cap, busted hip and a cane. I mean, it's not like we didn't give you a chance. . . .John Boy it's not working out.

JOHN

Brad, I'm back, ready to work. The firm has an investment in me and . . .

BRAD

(*Interrupting*) My point, my point exactly. Investment's gone sour. Got to cut our losses.

JOHN

Hey, I'll do anything.

BRAD

Yeah, yeah, sure. But we gotta watch it. One more month and you're off probation, a regular associate so to speak, severance and all that.

JOHN

Research. Must be some of that.

BRAD

No point making you a regular when you're excess baggage already.

JOHN

Write some memoranda of law for you, for the firm?

BRAD

Memor-Raandah-of-Law! Haw, haw. Shit! "I was out of paper and there being no grass, I used your memo to wipe my ass."

JOHN

Huh?

BRAD

Got that from an ole boy in construction. Asked me some question and I researched my butt off, wrote him this long memo and he sends my bill back, unpaid, with that small notation. "I was out of paper and there being no grass, . . ." Haw, haw, haw.

JOHN

But Brad, you were right, . . .

BRAD

"Right?!" "Right," for Chrissake? Who gives a shit about being "right?" I was fucking poor! Not coddled like you guys are, huge starting salaries, bennies up the ass. Hell no, all those years, cubby-hole office, chasing ambulances, bribing bail bondsmen and paramedics to scatter my cards around. Hard times, man! Wife . . . When out of the fuckin blue, I get a shot at this golden guy in construction . . . and I blow it. I get limericks for green. How the hell was I "right"?

JOHN

I see what you mean Brad, but a lawyer has to do research, find out what the law is? What other way is there?

BRAD

You stick your neck out. Like this, see. You stick your neck out. I see where Murray didn't really train you at all. Shouldn't hafta explain this. (Pause) Look, right or wrong, a lawyer's gotta be creative; you gotta invent, embroider, lull with your voice. . . . It's a game.

JOHN

I thought it was a profession.

BRAD

Don't get hooked by the hype, fella. Wife OK?

JOHN

What?

BRAD

Sometimes hard to tell, right?

JOHN

I suppose . . .

BRAD

Especially when you're clocking the hours. Never home. Remember too well.

JOHN

Your wife?

BRAD

Yeah, that too. Working. Working. Home late. Fagged . . . Hard to tell about a wife.

JOHN

Wouldn't know, I'm not married Brad. You know that.

BRAD

Aw, it's the same thing. You and Ellen, living together.

JOHN

We don't live together, not yet anyway.

BRAD

No kidding? Thought you did. Well, you oughta get moving there John Boy, before somebody else does.

JOHN

You think so.

BRAD

Sure, she's a dish. But she ain't dreaming baby shoes, she's a fuckin first class lawyer. You should see her hours! We make mondo moola on her work!

JOHN

I wouldn't know. We never, never, discuss work.

BRAD

What?

JOHN

I never even know what she's working on.

BRAD

No shit.

JOHN

A rule with us.

BRAD

Yeah?

JOHN

Iron-clad. Zero.

BRAD

Amazing.

JOHN

Her rule, not mine.

BRAD

No kidding. . . .Yeah, well she is sort of . . .

JOHN

Sort of what, Brad?

BRAD
Oh, you know, private. Her rule, huh?

JOHN
Yeah.

BRAD
And you two almost living together.

JOHN
We see a certain amount of each other.

BRAD
Sure you do. A large certain amount, I bet. Weekends! Oh those once-in-a-blue moon weekends! Week nights don't count for lawyers anyway, everyone's too fuckin pooped. If you can even get home, that is. But, oh, those occasional weekends! Am I right? Am I ever right! With a few necessary adjustments for casts and things. Haw, haw!

JOHN
(Silence) What's Ellen got to do with this, Brad? I thought . . .

BRAD
(Interrupting) "You thought"! You fucking "thought"! "What's-Ellen-got to-do-with-all-this?"! You're making me feel unwanted, hurried. In my own goddamn law firm. You're fired, John Boy!

JOHN
What?

BRAD
Canned, sacked, caput, finished . . . fucking fired. I want you to get your shit outta here this weekend. This weekend, got it?

JOHN
Jesus! No notice, no warning? No explanation?

BRAD

Whatta think we've been doing, last few minutes?

JOHN

Look, Brad, I know this is a difficult time at the firm. But goddammit, I need this job, I really need it. Paying off my education. I got rent. But it's more than that, I want to be a part of this firm.

BRAD

Yeah. Well, we all want to belong, John Boy, and everybody's got debts and rent. Or mortgages. Personally, I got huge mortgage motion on the white elephant in the country.

JOHN

This isn't fair, Brad. I just got back.

BRAD

You know what I'm gonna say.

JOHN

Life isn't fair, I know. But, Jesus, this leg and . . .

BRAD

Yeah, if I'd known I'd have tended to this earlier and saved the load on our medical policy but . . . Well, your good luck.

JOHN

But you've got some control, some discretion.

BRAD

Hands are tied, John Boy. What can I do? You're a maverick, you're a . . . unnh, Japanese . . .

JOHN

Japanese?

BRAD

Movies, the movies! This guy, this Jap guy, this warrior, loses his lord, his leader, whatever. And ever after he and all his gang of associated warriors, samurai guys, wander from pillar to pole, shit on and starving and unable to find anyone who'll take 'em in and feed 'em and pay 'em to strut around in skirts cutting people up. What the hell do they call 'em?

JOHN

Ronin.

BRAD

What?

JOHN

Ronin. They're called ronin.

BRAD

Ronin! That's it!

JOHN

Seriously, Brad, you know what it's like out there.

BRAD

Ronin! You got it, John Boy, good for you!

JOHN

The world's crawling with unemployed lawyers now. And thirty, forty thousand new ones popping out each year.

BRAD

Ronin, yeah.

JOHN

Milling around trying to find work.

BRAD

Untouchables, lost their lord and castle and all connection with society. Haw, haw! Love those movies. Course it's not funny.

JOHN

Give me a chance, for Christ's sake. I'll make it up to you.

BRAD

Ro . . . Yeah? Whatta ya mean "chance"? (BRAD's *cell phone rings.*)
Hello, hello. Who? (*Deferentially*) Oh, Buster, Bussturr, what can I
. . . What? The tax thing, yeah, yeah, yeah. Look Buster . . . What?
(*His hand over the phone*) Gimme your phone. Can't hear a fucking
thing on this piece of junk.

JOHN

Brad, I don't have a phone, not yet.

BRAD

Shit! How the hell you expect to be a lawyer without a phone?
(*Into the cell phone*) Hold on, Buster, can't hear you. I'll call you
right back from my office. (*Going out the door*) Give you a chance,
huh? I'll be back.

Blackout.

Scene Four

Noon the same day. BRAD *and* ELLEN *are seated at a table in a restaurant.*

BRAD

(Pause) Old times, eh?

ELLEN

This is business, right? McFarland.

BRAD

Well, you oughtta know.

ELLEN

What?

BRAD

You're the one wanted to meet.

ELLEN

At the firm.

BRAD

Heavy schedule there.

ELLEN

So, you said lunch.

BRAD

And here we are. . . . Ellie, Ellie. Business. Of course it's business. McFarland. And that ties in with some other things I want to cover too, concerning you.

ELLEN

What's that?

BRAD

Later, later.

ELLEN

Not so good at waiting. You know that.

BRAD

Oh, yeah. How well I remember.

ELLEN

Time you forgot.

BRAD

"You know that" / "Time you forgot." On/off. Up/down. You happy here?

ELLEN

Here?

BRAD

Yeah. At the firm.

ELLEN

Sure. Happy as any other overworked lawyer, I guess. You saying there's a problem? My work?

BRAD

No. No problem there. Your work's OK, better than OK. And you look wonderful. I can say that, can't I? Attest that the grind at B,T&T hasn't turned you into a tough old cow?

ELLEN

Thanks.

BRAD

Some outfit.

ELLEN

Nothing special.

BRAD

Knockout stuff.

ELLEN

Maybe I guessed the Managing Partner might like expensive restaurants.

BRAD

How would you have guessed that.

ELLEN

Yeah, how.

BRAD

(Pause) Friends?

ELLEN

(Pause) Sure. Friends. Just wanted to be sure we're talking about the same case.

BRAD

Hey, it's over, I know that. You've got new friends, new friend. But we can't deny the past. Know what I mean.

ELLEN

Sounds reasonable. But so does "Give him an inch and he'll take a mile."

BRAD

C'mon, Ellie. Not fair.

ELLEN

Just keeping up my guard.

BRAD

Past is with us, Ellie. Like it or not. Proust and the macaroon, . . .

ELLEN

How's that?

                    BRAD
Unhh, Proust and the macaroon.

                    ELLEN
Marcel and the madeleine?

                    BRAD
Whatever.

                    ELLEN
Believe me, it's a distinction with a difference.

                    BRAD
OK. But you know what I mean.

                    ELLEN
I know, but since when do you know?

                    BRAD
Unhhh, I've got this video course in literature.

                    ELLEN
No kidding. What for?

                    BRAD
To watch, learn, what else?

                    ELLEN
When, while you're on the throne?

                    BRAD
Shouldn't ridicule my better impulses.

                    ELLEN
No.

                    BRAD
I'm serious.

ELLEN

You are?

BRAD

Yeah. I'm trying to broaden out.

ELLEN

Given your expense account, places like this, shouldn't be hard.

BRAD

My mind, Ellie. My interests.

ELLEN

Oh? What brought this on?

BRAD

(*Pause*) Seems like the firm's all I care about doesn't it, Ellie? Billings, the law, working flat-out. Well, that's not the whole book on me. Look, I realize, I've always realized there's something else out there. Better, higher things. Books, art . . .

ELLEN

Go on.

BRAD

Poetry, stories . . . children.

ELLEN

Brad! You've met some nice girl, a nice old-fashioned girl!

BRAD

Jesus! Of course not.

ELLEN

No, suppose not.

BRAD

Hey, I'm serious. I'm trying to explain a change, in myself.

ELLEN

Sorry. That is serious.

BRAD

And you're responsible, really.

ELLEN

Uh oh.

BRAD

Among the other things I thank you for. Many things.

ELLEN

And I thought it was all physical.

BRAD

That too, for godsake. Of course!

ELLEN

Jesus, Ellie. Go figure!

BRAD

You know how I felt about all that, why . . .

ELLEN

No, Brad, no! Strike it, strike it! I shouldn't have brought it up, shouldn't have joked.

BRAD

Ellie, oh God, you were . . .

ELLEN

Cut, cut, cut!

BRAD

OK. Right. I know. But, Ellie, like now, right now, it's noon. Remember, remember then?

ELLEN

C'mon, Brad.

BRAD

Rain pouring down, windows all streaked and steamy. I'd rush back
to the apartment after teaching my class. Outside cold and nasty
but inside, . . . And after, lying there in the bed with you, listening
to the rain, that's the best there is. . . . Like it was yesterday.

ELLEN

Another life is more like it.

BRAD

I loved those afternoons. Loved the whole thing. . . .

ELLEN

C'mon, Brad. . . . Listen, I'm not saying I hated it. But it's over, been
over for ages.

BRAD

When you left. Morning you packed that old clunker and drove off.
Know what I did?

ELLEN

No. Don't want to.

BRAD

Just stood there, couldn't move, watching till you were out of sight,
round the corner, gone. Then I went back inside and crawled in
bed. All my clothes on, suit, tie, everything, didn't even take off my
shoes. It was still warm, still smelled sweet, like you. Suddenly I
started sobbing, for chrissake. Couldn't stop. And I never cry. Never.

ELLEN

(*Long pause*) We better talk business. OK?

BRAD

OK. Yeah. Yeah. OK.

ELLEN

McFarland Construction.

BRAD

Pretty impressive, huh?

ELLEN

McFarland?

BRAD

McFarland. Buster's empire.

ELLEN

I . . .

BRAD

There's a lesson in it.

ELLEN

Maybe, yes, I see one too but . . .

BRAD

Important lesson. Pay you to remember.

ELLEN

What?

BRAD

In the struggle of life, in the grand arena of the law, among law firms, within a single firm, one can do it! Know what I mean.

ELLEN

One?

BRAD

One! One client. The right client, just one, you can build to the sky. That's what McFarland's been. What a beautiful cash cow!

ELLEN

I know how much you've put into it.

BRAD

You got no idea. Nobody does!

ELLEN

No, of course not. But I can imagine.

BRAD

Don't imagine. Only remember! One! One can do it. Only remember!

ELLEN

(*Pause*) Brad, I've been going over McFarland's financials.

BRAD

Good, good.

ELLEN

Wouldn't call what I found good. For starters take corporate house-keeping, what lousy records, blank minute books. And, Jesus, those subs. I mean if you're General Counsel, I think you'd better begin taking a closer look.

BRAD

Hey, Buster loves us.

ELLEN

But should we, should you, love him?

BRAD

Whadda ya mean?

ELLEN

Cows dry up sometimes, even cash cows.

BRAD

Yeah? You think so? About Buster. No shit! Cows dry up. Well, look who's talking!

ELLEN

What's that supposed to mean?

BRAD

I'm the goddamn Managing Partner, you're the associate. Don't go telling me about my best client until you've rebuilt a firm like Biggins & Tostick and put your own name on the end. After that, you can lecture me on clients and billings. I wrote the fucking book, know what I mean.

ELLEN

But you haven't been reading Buster's books and I have, right?

BRAD

So?

ELLEN

I know how you feel about him, Brad, but the guy looks strung out to me.

BRAD

(Pause) Ah, OK, I get it. Look, Ellie, something you gotta understand about Buster, he's always on the edge. And he always muddles through. Besides, McFarland's got B,T&T, the best advice. We see to that.

ELLEN

Maybe, but has he followed it?

BRAD

The golden touch. He could charm Attila the Fucking Hun.

ELLEN

All I'm saying, he may have to. I think the empire's upside down.

BRAD

The bankers. Last year.

ELLEN

Yeah?

BRAD

Suddenly unfriendly. Threatening to call loans, cut off lines of credit. Disaster loomed. Buster and I meet with 'em and after he talks for a few minutes they open up like one of those little paper Japanese things you drop in a glass of water and a goddamn flag comes out. They end up trying to give him more money. Magician. He's a goddamn magician. And when Buster gets the money he uses it to make mondo moola, for himself, for us. What's wrong with that? Where's the harm?

ELLEN

You know what I'm going to say, Brad.

BRAD

Yeah, I know, course sometimes he doesn't tell all. But what the hell, nobody does that.

ELLEN

Nobody?

BRAD

We're talking serious people, Ellie, not goody-two-shoes. The operators, the ones who aim high, build big. They know how to use the pedals, emphasize the positive, muffle the rest. Like a trial.

ELLEN

I guess what I'm worried about is the verdict.

BRAD

Ellie, something basic. Blocking and tackling. Know what I mean. (*Pause*) If you're going to play in the big time, represent people like Buster, you got to talk the same lingo, think the same. That's the only way to stay in the game. Trust me. (*Silence*) And, well, after all this bullshit, there's something else. Worrying about McFarland's financial health is like worrying about last year's Super Bowl. It's too fucking late. We bought in. For us, he's it. To do McFarland's work, we expanded, hired new people . . .

ELLEN

I know, Brad, I know. But denying . . .

BRAD

OK. Let me bring it closer to home. Take your friend there, the kid, what's-his-name, John Boy.

ELLEN

His name is John Botz and he's no kid.

BRAD

Sure, sure. A real stud. But when it comes to B,T&T, without Murray, he's road kill. . . . Unless, of course, there's some McFarland work for him. So, you ought to speak kindly of Buster on that ground alone, right? Know what I mean.

ELLEN

I confess I really wasn't looking at Buster, or McFarland, in that light. . . . What I'm saying, I don't like the looks of the McFarland stuff you gave me, especially McFarland Marine, the subsidiary. The sale of that barge in Brazil, if it ever took place, there or anywhere else . . .

BRAD

I know, I know, minutes. You need minutes.

ELLEN

I mean, is this a valid, functioning corporation going by the book or do they just make it all up when they have to file tax returns?

BRAD

OK, so you need some minutes of directors' meetings showing that the barge sale, other stuff, was approved by the board, done by the numbers.

ELLEN

And done at the right time.

BRAD

Sure. . . . What's the date again?

ELLEN

Brad! The date is the date they did it. Whatever the minutes say.
I'm not about to vacation courtesy of the Feds because I made stuff
up in a tax case.

BRAD

I'll get you minutes.

ELLEN

It isn't only the minutes. It's other stuff too.

BRAD

(*Pause*) But you admit you don't have all the facts.

ELLEN

Nobody ever has *all* the facts.

BRAD

See? So let's not get all excited. Ellie, as a friend. With affection
and, well, hope. Ellie, Ellie, Ellie. Don't make the "dumb associate's
mistake," worrying about things you haven't been asked to worry
about. Number one, there's no time for that bullshit if you're going
to keep up the pace. Number two, you're not the client's priest,
you're his mouthpiece. You're on his side, his buddy on the bloody
sea of business. Don't try to find what's wrong with a client. Build
him up, find out what he wants and do it. Answer the questions
you've been asked. Period. End of argument. End of case.

ELLEN

Is that so?

BRAD

Yeah, absolutely. Don't worry where it's all leading. That'll be the next case. . . . If you can't do this, you'll never pay the bills. You might as well be a social worker, yeah, or go into religion. So keep the goddamn ball in play, for chrissake. Especially this one. *(Pause)* Look, forgetting all this other shit, can you handle the McFarland tax thing? I know, I know, you need some minutes. If you get 'em?

ELLEN

Well, if you have minutes and they show the directors made the right moves, yeah, I think I can handle it.

BRAD

Great. I'll get you the minutes. Now, next case. You busy this weekend?

ELLEN

Say again?

BRAD

You've got plans. I know, I know. The kid, what's his name, John-Boy, just back, no doubt horny as hell and all that but let me put it this way: It's a career move. Know what I mean.

ELLEN

Brad, you spilled wine on your tie.

BRAD

Whaa? Shit! . . . Where? I don't see any.

ELLEN

Thought you did.

BRAD

Really like this tie.

ELLEN

Yeah, it's very nice. Bold. Where'd you get it?

BRAD

Where was I?

ELLEN

And the coat, umm, suit, coat. Striking.

BRAD

New. Where . . . ? Oh yeah, we were talking about this weekend.

ELLEN

I don't believe this.

BRAD

Huh?

ELLEN

You're actually telling me it would be good for my career if I spent the weekend at your place? With you?

BRAD

Yeah. Yeah. Believe me. It would. I guarantee it. Why? (*Pause*) Oh, Jesus! I see. No, no. I mean you got it wrong, totally wrong. Buster's coming over and, hey, you'll be safe as in God's pocket.

ELLEN

No kidding? You trading that tie for a round collar after lunch? God's pocket, huh?

BRAD

Safer than. Kathleen's.

ELLEN

Who?

BRAD

You don't remember?

ELLEN

Remember what?

BRAD

Mentioned her a lot.

ELLEN

What's her name again?

BRAD

Kathleen, Kathleen Thomas.

ELLEN

Oh Brad, it's a nice Catholic girl. You old sly goat, you secretly married a nice Catholic girl!

BRAD

Mother of God! Hardly.

ELLEN

No, I suppose not. This Kathleen your cook?

BRAD

That too. No, mother. Kathleen is my mother. I . . . The Mother sort of lives with me. For the time being. In the country.

ELLEN

Oh.

BRAD

You see why there's no problem. What could happen?

ELLEN

Huh?

BRAD

My mother. She'll be there.

ELLEN

You live with your mother?

BRAD

Backwards.

ELLEN

Pardon?

BRAD

You got it backwards.

ELLEN

Got what backwards?

BRAD

She lives with me.

ELLEN

You live together.

BRAD

The Mother lives with me, temporarily. You said I lived with her.

ELLEN

Now that does sound to me like a distinction without a difference. Still, any way you want to put it, it's very interesting.

BRAD

The point is, she'll be there.

ELLEN

So I have nothing to worry about, over the weekend.

BRAD

Exactly. My mother, Ellie. It's The Mother. What could happen to you with The Enforcer in your corner? She's a shark of a chaperon. Ruined my adolescence. Know what I mean.

ELLEN

Your mother?

BRAD

Trust me, Ellie, I'm not going to even look at you the wrong way with my mother there. Much as I might like to.

ELLEN

You're serious about this?

BRAD

Absolutely. Look, it'd be good for the firm, for the firm's relationship with its best client, and good for your career. I can tell my partners you know Buster, President of MacFarland.

ELLEN

Buster's coming, huh?

BRAD

What I'm saying. Bubbles might too but I doubt it. Seems she's spending a lot of time elsewhere these days, traveling mostly, I guess. What the hell, she can afford it and ole Buster, he doesn't complain, haw, haw. Anyhow, we'll play some golf and . . .

ELLEN

Golf? I haven't played four complete rounds since I came to work here. Besides, the forecast isn't . . .

BRAD

Then we'll do backgammon. Mere possibility of playing with a beautiful low handicap like you will make him feel great. And you'll have fun, believe me.

ELLEN

Let me think about it, Brad. Not a lot of notice.

BRAD

Sure.

BRAD

Business, Ellie, that's because it's business. With Buster, it's good to move fast. Meanwhile I'll arrange those minutes for you.

Blackout.

Scene Five

Thursday night, JOHN's "office." CHARLIE is emptying the boxes containing ERNIE's things onto a table. SPEEDBALL is in her cage on the table.

CHARLIE

(Sorting through ERNIE's stuff) Tomorrow, Speedball, tomorrow, if the weather's OK. And when I launch you, go home, straight home. Hawks live in these tall buildings. So climb fast, circle a couple of times and get the hell out. OK?

JOHN enters, unseen by CHARLIE.

JOHN

OK! My sentiments exactly.

CHARLIE

Ahh, *bon soir.* I thought you'd gone.

JOHN

Buona sera. Naw, just wandering around the firm after dark, hoping someone would throw some work at me. But I seem to be invisible. . . . Thought we were going to play dominoes.

CHARLIE

Had another call from Ernie's sister this afternoon. Boom chickee boom. Think I better sort his stuff tonight. Sorry.

JOHN

Doesn't matter. Day like today, I'd probably have lost my ass. *(At SPEEDBALL's cage)* Speedball, if I had your wings, I'd split so fast.

CHARLIE

The musty scent of disenchantment?

JOHN

Black mood, for sure.

CHARLIE

C'mon, hang around. I'd like the company.

JOHN

I'm lousy company tonight.

CHARLIE

Hey, cheer up. If you can just find a way to return to the insane pace of lawyering, your malaise will disappear. You'll feel customarily numb again.

JOHN

Charlie, I gotta split.

CHARLIE

Don't rush off. (Pause) OK, to be honest, I want company, your company.

JOHN

You want company, I want work.

CHARLIE

This is different. I'm a little anxious, afraid.

JOHN

So what's different? I'm scared too.

CHARLIE

It's Ernie. Ernie might show up.

JOHN

Jesus, Ernie, again? The lurking harbinger of my fate.

CHARLIE

His sister's worried, very worried. Says he's, umm, "fixated," is how she put it.

JOHN

Fixated on what, who?

CHARLIE

On this firm, specifically on Brad. She thinks Ernie's planning to come here. Told her to tell him I'd have his stuff at my place in the country. Better if he doesn't come to the firm.

JOHN

You'll have to handle Ernie alone, Charlie. I'm outta here.

CHARLIE

He thinks Brad stole this stuff. Pretty funny, huh? Brad would trash it instantly. But I saved it.

JOHN

Good for you. Ernie can't blame you for that.

CHARLIE

He can do anything. I remember feeling that way. . . . Says he's got a gun.

JOHN

Oh, oh. Charlie, these kooks never get the right guy, the one they're after.

CHARLIE

Chickee boom. Shotgun, she says.

JOHN

Shit! Or they get five or six others too.

CHARLIE

He was the least violent of persons . . . but you never know. I well remember my own black thoughts.

JOHN

(Starting to leave) Yeah, well, I hate to abandon you but I'm not about to die for Brad's sins. I really am outta here.

CHARLIE

Don't worry, John, it's late, building's locked. C'mon, I just need company, stay a while anyhow.

JOHN

(*Stops at* SPEEDBALL's *cage*) But, come to think of it, this is just what I need.

CHARLIE

Pigeons? You want to get into pigeons, John? I got pigeons' mother. I could sell you a starter kit very reasonably. A pair of blue bars, maybe one of tumblers. You know tumblers?

JOHN

Charlie, Charlie, . . .

CHARLIE

Homers are great, the backbone of the fleet, but tumblers, oh my god, tumblers are beautiful. Funny too. And they perform at home, you don't have to take them away somewhere to see if they can find their way back. Tumblers, you let tumblers out and they climb and climb till you can hardly see 'em. Suddenly they tip over and fall head-over-heels straight down through the sky until they pull out at the last minute right over your head. Thrilling.

JOHN

Makes me airsick to think about it. Shit, all I need now is pigeons. Cage, Charlie, a cage! What I want is a cage. Here.

CHARLIE

In the office? Why?

JOHN

Well, for Giorgio.

CHARLIE

What? Who's Giorgio?

                        JOHN
I got this . . . umm, rat.

                        CHARLIE
Rat! Rats kill squabs, suck eggs, spread disease. Hate rats.

                        JOHN
And here you are, working in a law firm.

                        CHARLIE
That lame joke! When'd you get this rat?

                        JOHN
When I went to get my yogurt for lunch.

                        CHARLIE
Yeah?

                        JOHN
Bought him from a kid on the street.

                        CHARLIE
So, where is he?

                        JOHN
(JOHN produces GIORGIO from his inside coat pocket.) You'll like
him. Has character. (CHARLIE inspects GIORGIO, visually.) Most
of the time, just dozes, exhausted, had a lot of responsibility lately .
. . another story. I really don't mind him in my pocket but not a good
long-term solution. Climbs out. While ago I reached over to open a
drawer and he fell down my sleeve into the shitcan.

                        CHARLIE
I think I got something. (CHARLIE rummages around and gives
JOHN a disassembled cage.)

                        JOHN
Thanks, . . . I guess. What is it?

CHARLIE

Cage, broken down. Everything's there. All you have to do is put it together. While I'm parsing Ernie's past.

JOHN

(Beginning to put the cage together) How'd I ever get into this law thing anyway?

CHARLIE

Aw, probably like a lot of us: Bewildered college senior, for lack of a better idea, and terrified of going to work, wanders into law school.

JOHN

Visions of learning, prestige, the enlightened exercise of power . . . and, of course, a living wage.

CHARLIE

Under the delusion it's still a civilized profession allowing for a modicum of leisure and culture.

JOHN

Some writing on the side.

CHARLIE

Heh, heh. The arts, travel.

JOHN

Yeah. *(Pause)* Listen, Charlie, don't get the wrong idea, what I'm going to say. I still want to be a lawyer, all that, here, at B,T&T.

CHARLIE

But what?

JOHN

In hospital, the ward, this high school kid, Tom, in the next bed. . . . Eight o'clock one morning they roll him out for some routine surgery. Two hours later, they're back for his iPod and clothes. Died on the operating table. I'm horrified. I really liked him, girlfriend too, she came every day, brought me things. Now he's gone, had no time at all, barely got started. That afternoon I glance over as the light is slanting across his empty bed and I get it, the obvious. His bed is my bed. Sooner or later. . . .

CHARLIE

"Do not send to find for whom . . ."

JOHN

And what the fuck will I have done? How will I have spent my time? Will my life add up to a shelf of SEC registrations like Murray's? Or one full of trial transcripts like Brad's? Beautifully bound volumes no one will ever open again. Little tombstones. Lying there I realize that for years I haven't been thinking at all, let alone living. Law school, it's not school, it's boot camp. Conditioning, like Skinner's pigeons, Pavlov's dog. Trains people to forget themselves, forget that we only have so long. In the name of this great abstraction called The Law. Money, that too. And, yeah, Power . . . But when you crawl into the mouth of the labyrinth, you forget there's no thread to follow out, no escape, because to understand what's happening to you, you'd have to break the pace, do some self-examination. And you're afraid to break the pace.

CHARLIE

Do not stop or slow down.

JOHN

Right! Or look back. First month, you learn not to look back. From there on, it's all inertia, dumb momentum. And fear, fear too. I mean, one year of law school's worth nothing. So you go for two which gets you in deeper and still is worth nothing. After three you may have a degree but you're not a lawyer till you pass the bar. So you take the cram course and let's say you pass first time.

CHARLIE

Now you're a "lawyer" but you've never done it, don't know anything about practice.

JOHN

Right! You're so theoretical you're virtually invisible, an out-of-body experiment.

CHARLIE

With a desperate need to prove you haven't wasted all those years.

JOHN

Now it's time to "pay your dues," get some experience, practice a few years.

CHARLIE

Then you'll be a real lawyer, and well, there'll always be plenty of time to decide whether you want to keep doing it. Heh, heh.

JOHN

So after the bar, if you're, umm, lucky, you become an associate and start all over again, in a brand new race to make partner some day. By now who questions anything? Been whanging on the same gong so long, can't stop. Gong-sound is what keeps you going, all you know.

CHARLIE

A life on rails, careering toward a vanishing point that's always just beyond the picture plane.

JOHN

End of story.

CHARLIE

Story? (*Chuckles*) What story? Lawyers scuttle over the surface of life telling other people's stories, never their own. A fortiori, after death their shapeless souls drift eternally through the ether searching for the lives they never invented. Sad, sad, a great waste. What untold stories, what unlived lives, such unmade souls. . . . *Quelles tragédies.*

JOHN

Charlie, I'm serious.

CHARLIE

Sorry.

JOHN

(*Pause*) Actually, I'm done. And I feel better. Thanks for letting me spew my sour grapes.

CHARLIE

Anytime, John. Anytime.

JOHN

(*Pause*) You still painting?

CHARLIE

In the country, all the time.

JOHN

(*Pause*) What really happened to you, here at the firm? If you want to say.

CHARLIE

I was chief assistant for Mr. Tostick, big anti-trust case, the old firm, Biggins & Tostick, long time ago. Ignored warning signs, kept working. One morning I couldn't get out of bed. All my systems had shut down.

JOHN

Jesus, terrible!

CHARLIE

Not pleasant. Still it saved my life, brought it all home to me, the obvious, as you were saying . . .

JOHN

But you'd been this red hot lawyer, destined for greatness. Then when you come back, you're filing stuff, making office assignments. I mean, what about ambition, recognition . . .

CHARLIE

Fame, fortune, the love of beautiful women. Power. By then they seemed transitory, superficial . . . in the end, morbid. (*Pause*) Besides, . . . you won't tell?

JOHN

Huh? Of course not.

CHARLIE

I'm going to make it as a painter.

JOHN

Ahh.

CHARLIE

(Looking at GIORGIO's *cage)* Wait, we can do better than that.

JOHN

Charlie, don't worry. This is a palace.

CHARLIE

But cold, unfurnished. Take him out for a minute. *(Spreading some shredded paper in the cage)* There.

JOHN

Rat heaven. Thanks, Charlie. *(Putting* GIORGIO *back in his cage)*

CHARLIE

Better, huh, *Giorgio?* Rat's nest of shredded legal documents. The metaphors clamor for attention. On the level of your limp joke, John. . . . Hey! I got one more. A wheel. You gotta get the goddamn rat a wheel.

JOHN

Brilliant!

CHARLIE

Every lawyer must have one.

JOHN

Irregardless of race, sex, color or religion!

CHARLIE

"Irregardless" is not a word!

JOHN

I think it's become one. Anyway, whadda you expect, I'm not an English teacher, I'm a lawyer? *(Pause)* If I can find some work, that is. Hey, c'mon Charlie, suggest something? Anything, I don't care what. Handling traffic tickets for some client's wife, sitting with a bank officer waiting to testify before the grand jury, filing papers. Nothing's too low. You must have something.

CHARLIE

John, I told you. Nothing much comes my way, certainly nothing suitable has.

JOHN

Suitable? Who gives a shit about suitable, Charlie. I'm fighting for my life around here. Anything! Anything at all. Fuck "suitable."

CHARLIE

Nothing, John. Should have said "nothing" because I have nothing, really.

JOHN

Witness changes his story.

CHARLIE

What?

JOHN

Nothing, nothing. C'mon, let's go.

(JOHN *covers the cage and puts it behind the filing cabinet.*)

JOHN *and* CHARLIE *exit.*

Blackout.

SCENE SIX

JOHN's *office the following morning, Friday.*

The lights come up on JOHN *at his desk as* BRAD's *footsteps are heard offstage.*

BRAD *enters angrily.*

                    JOHN
Brad!

                    BRAD
Give you a chance, my ass! What did I get for it?

                    JOHN
For what?

                    BRAD
Don't play dumb with me, John Boy.

                    JOHN
Brad, honest to God, . . .

                    BRAD
Minor corporate housekeeping . . . *(Pulling papers from his coat pocket and waving them)* All I wanted, all I fucking asked.

                    JOHN
Housekeeping?

                    BRAD
(Putting the papers back in his pocket) Routine, run-of-the-bleeding-mill corporate stuff, simple minutes of board of directors, something a dumb paralegal could do with her eyes closed, for chrissake and . . .

                    JOHN
Wait . . .

BRAD

And you refuse, you fucking refuse!

JOHN

Brad, I swear, . . .

BRAD

The goddamn nerve!

JOHN

I don't know anything about this.

BRAD

It won't work, John Boy.

JOHN

I never got anything. Look, see for yourself. My desk is clean, nothing.

BRAD

The nothing kid. Yeah, you got nothing because you wouldn't take it.

JOHN

Take what?

BRAD

Not good enough for you, huh? Not up to Murray's standards?

JOHN

Brad, I've been begging for work. I mean, ask Charlie, for godsake.

BRAD

Charlie! That tears it, John Boy! Charlie! (*Getting up*) Shit, how do you think I know all this?

JOHN

I don't know. Know what?

BRAD

Chickee chickee boom chickee, John Boy. "Chick chickee boom" himself.

JOHN

Charlie?

BRAD

Your old pal, right? I gave it to him to give to you yesterday.

JOHN

What did Charlie say?

BRAD

Charlie say, John Boy doesn't like *Il Duce's* work assignments.

JOHN

Charlie said that?

BRAD

So I find your assignment on my desk this morning, when the god-damn thing should be done already. (BRAD's *cell phone rings.*) Hello. What? Who? . . . Oh, Buster, yeah, tomorrow. In the country. We're going out there tonight. We'll brief you on it tomorrow. What? . . . The stuff's in my office, Buster. (*Walking out of* JOHN's *office*) Hold on while I go back there. What? Oh, yeah, I agree, I agree entirely.

BRAD *exits.*

(JOHN *immediately begins pounding on the floor with the head of his cane.*)

JOHN

Charlie! Goddammit, Charlie!

CHARLIE

(*Offstage, as* JOHN *keeps pounding*) Hold on, John. I'm coming, I'm coming.

Blackout.

Act Two

SCENE SEVEN

JOHN, on a darkened stage, is still pounding on the floor with his cane as the lights come up on CHARLIE running into his office, out of breath.

CHARLIE

For godsake John, you OK? You fall?

JOHN

Fall! I was fucking tripped.

CHARLIE

I thought you fell down or something.

JOHN

How the hell could you?

CHARLIE

Boom chickee . . . How could I what?

JOHN

You told Brad I wouldn't take the work he gave you for me to do, for chrissake! And you tell him I call him *Il Duce*.

CHARLIE

Where'd you get all this, John?

JOHN

Brad! Where the hell you think? Just now.

CHARLIE

You believe I'd do things like that? Yesterday afternoon, late, Brad came in with some stuff pertaining to a McFarland subsidiary, min-ute book, handwritten notes. He told me to tell you to take care of it. I looked it over and told him he'd have to give it to you himself.

CENTER: JOHN

So what the hell was wrong with it? Where do you get off? I mean, how the hell do you arrogate to yourself the right to decide whether some associate gets work the Managing Partner wants to give him?

CENTER: CHARLIE

You're very angry with me, aren't you?

CENTER: JOHN

You're goddamn right! I'm fucking furious. I've been betrayed. Again. It sure as shit isn't one big family, Charlie. You, even you!

CENTER: CHARLIE

As for the *Il Duce* assertion, of course I never told him you call him that. You may remember my telling you last night that I'd forget the appellation, if I were you.

CENTER: JOHN

Yeah. If? If! See, Charlie, the thing is, you're not me! And I'd like the right to decide for myself whether I want to do work that the fucking Managing Partner assigns me. Jesus, you know how hard I'm trying to hang on around here. . . . You assume too much, Charlie.

CENTER: CHARLIE

And a lawyer should never assume.

CENTER: JOHN

You've been here so long you think you know it all, making decisions that affect other people.

CENTER: CHARLIE

Meddling old fool, huh? Well, maybe. . . . Maybe not. Boom chickee boom.

CHARLIE *exits.*

Blackout.

Scene Eight

BRAD *enters as the lights come up on* JOHN *in his office.*

JOHN
Brad! Listen, I had it out with Charlie.

BRAD
Had it out, huh?

JOHN
Hell yes. I mean I don't know what he was thinking of. Whatever you need, I'll do it.

BRAD
Maybe you just didn't realize how serious things are? You think if I gave you this job, it'd turn out satisfactory?

JOHN
I do.

BRAD
I'd be pleasantly surprised?

JOHN
I promise you.

BRAD
Scout's honor?

JOHN
Scout's honor!

BRAD
Into the teeth of the gale?

JOHN

Into the heart of the storm.

BRAD

Lock and load?

JOHN

Bayonets fixed.

BRAD

Charge?

JOHN

Over the top!

BRAD

No questions asked?

JOHN

Your wish is my command.

BRAD

John Boy, I don't know why I'm doing this. Against all my principles but I'm going to give you a chance to save your ass, right here at BT&T.

JOHN

Brad, you won't be sorry.

BRAD

That's my boy, John Boy.

JOHN

What'd you give Charlie anyway?

BRAD

Shit, he didn't even tell you?

JOHN

No.

> BRAD

We go through this little bonding exercise just now, you didn't even know what you were talking about?

> JOHN

Huh?

> BRAD

Didn't even fucking know what you were promising to do! Shit . . . unless, of course, open-ended, saying you'd do whatever, whatever you got.

> JOHN

Whatever you give me.

> BRAD

Sure?

> JOHN

Sure.

> BRAD

Sign in blood?

> JOHN

Blood.

> BRAD

OK, on that oath, I'll tell you. It's a simple little thing for McFarland Construction.

> JOHN

McFarland Construction.

> BRAD

Ideal. The perfect test.

> JOHN

Of my work?

BRAD

Your seriousness, maturity.

JOHN

Right.

BRAD

Loyalty.

JOHN

What?

BRAD

To B,T&T.

JOHN

I see.

BRAD

To me.

JOHN

Oh.

BRAD

The perfect test.

JOHN

Brad, what's the McFarland matter?

BRAD

Very simple. Should appeal to you. We're talking imagination, cre-
ativity, inventiveness. Sure you want to try it?

JOHN

I need this job.

BRAD

Wouldn't see as much of Ellen, if you lost it. Right?

JOHN

That's the least of my problems right now, Brad.

BRAD

No kiddin? I bet she'd be surprised to hear that, haw, haw. Just kiddin . . . What we need are some minutes of a few meetings of a board of directors.

JOHN

Just give me notes about what went on at the meetings.

BRAD

What meetings?

JOHN

The meetings you want the minutes for.

BRAD

No meetings.

JOHN

No meetings?

BRAD

Nope. How could they? Didn't have enough directors. You gotta take care of that too.

JOHN

I do?

BRAD

Yeah. Got behind on elections. Only had a couple on the board. Not enough.

JOHN

No quorum?

BRAD

No board, really. But that's all taken care of here. (*Producing a sheet of paper*)

JOHN
You want minutes of no meetings, . . .

BRAD
Right.

JOHN
Of . . . of no board?

BRAD
You got it, John Boy.

JOHN
Brad, I don't think I understand. Or, if I do . . .

BRAD
Here we are, trying to get off to a good start, and you're cross-exam-
ining me and acting dumb, dragging your feet, foot, whatever.
. . . Look, just stick to the assignment: We need some corpo-
rate minutes, simple corporate minutes for McFarland Marine, a
McFarland subsidiary. You dig? (*Tossing the sheet of paper toward*
JOHN) There's everything we want in 'em, names of directors, reso-
lutions, dates of transactions and meetings, it's all down there.

JOHN
(*Looking at the paper*) "Bubbles?"

BRAD
Yeah, that's part of it. Barge, a barge named "Bubbles," it got sold.

JOHN
A barge named "Bubbles?"

BRAD
Right. Among other things the minutes have to show that the
board—the board you'll elect in the privacy of your new office
here—approved the sale of the barge, on the right date, at the right
place, like Brazil in October, not New Orleans in January. And get
'em to me tomorrow morning.

JOHN

You know tomorrow's Saturday.

BRAD

So it's Saturday. We got union work rules or something? I need 'em tomorrow. Playing golf with Buster Krause.

JOHN

Who's Buster Krause?

BRAD

Jesus! You weren't paying attention, John Boy! I told you. He's the limerick man.

JOHN

You said you lost him.

BRAD

I got him back. Yeah, actually you could learn from this. Very simple. I just found out what he'd like to hear, what he wanted to do. Know what I mean.

JOHN

Oh.

BRAD

Then I wrote another memorandum that somehow gave him the idea he could do what he wanted to do. After that he was glad to pay his bill. What's more, having got his way, he got into trouble and in no time he needed a lawyer again.

JOHN

But you'd told him . . .

BRAD

Sure, sure. That's what he said too, until I showed him my disclaimers, blessed boilerplate. Yessir, when I gave him a careful reading of my memo, he had to admit I'd never really said he could do what he wanted and also be absolutely safe. I mean, shit, no decent lawyer would ever say something that straight-forward. Anyhow, just then, damned if Buster's father-in-law, the founder of McFarland Construction, doesn't die. Believe me Buster's construction business was strictly the toy department compared to McFarland. So Buster's wife, Bubbles . . .

JOHN

She's the Bubbles?

BRAD

Yeah, the barge was named after her. She inherited control of the company and, bingo, Buster swung into action. Before you know it, with plenty of advice from you-know-who, Buster is President of McFarland Construction and B,T&T is General Counsel. The rest is history. End of lesson. Now, John Boy, I want a nice set of minutes for a very important client. Make sure the goods are delivered to my place in the country by ten hundred tomorrow morning.

JOHN

Country?

BRAD

Yeah? And use the messenger service. Don't come yourself.

JOHN

(Pause) You know what you're asking me to do?

BRAD

John Boy, sometimes you gotta stick your neck out for a client. And this piddling thing is nothin. Dumb little minutes, trivial corporate housekeeping for a wholly-owned subsidiary, for godsake. Really big deals, big money deals, are going down all the time. Three-card monte games like out on the street, except the sharks got Italian suits instead of tank tops and suites instead of tiny tables that fold up real quick. The world is never going to be saved, John Boy, it's just one huge shark tank, and you'll never make it out there if you let a little thing like reconstructing some minutes of a few lousy board meetings bother you. (Pause) Maybe we should forget the whole thing. Yeah, I think this wasn't a good idea.

JOHN

No, Brad, no . . . But look, even if it isn't a big deal, my problem is, uhh, the meetings aren't just "lousy," they're totally fictional, mythical even. Nothing ever took place, I'm not even "reconstructing," I'm, ummm, making it all . .

BRAD

I can't believe this. Haven't you ever heard of virtual reality or anything? What'd I tell you a while back about how a lawyer . . . a lawyer has got to be what, what John Boy? What does a lawyer gotta be?

JOHN

Creative?

BRAD

Creative. A lawyer has got to be creative. So be creative. (*Pause*) Look, just use the phrase, "as of." Know what I mean.

JOHN

"As of?"

BRAD

You write, "Minutes of the meeting of the Board of Directors held as of December 15th" or whatever, and so on. Jesus, do I gotta lead you by the hand? Here we are back at the real problem again! Who's going to give a shit anyway? Where's the harm? (*Pause*) OK, look, this'll make it clear even to you. A little story, personal experience. Know what I mean.

Here beginneth the lesson. I was just starting out and I had this P.I. case with great injuries but lousy facts. Before trial I happened to notice that certain documents, umm, bordering on crucial, hadn't been turned over to opposing counsel on discovery. Damned if I know how it happened. Probably some secretary goofed. Shit, I might have missed 'em myself, who knows. Anyhow, we go to trial and my client takes the stand and does some heavy lying, not unrelated to these very documents. Now, I was disturbed by all this, know what I mean.

JOHN
And if opposing counsel had had . . .

BRAD
Who's telling this anyway? . . . Like I said, I was disturbed by all
this. And the next day I had to make my closing argument, right?
Should I stop everything in it's tracks, or what? That night I'm walking up the street from Murphy's after spaghetti and a few beers,
worrying about the trial, what I'm going to do the next day when,
my God, this beautiful black chick passes me going the other way.
I can't take my eyes off her and I miss the fucking curb in the dark.
My briefcase, which is on the outswing gives me a nice take-off.
After a tremendous flight, I land in the middle of the street. On
my knees.

Jesus, the pain! The pain was unbelievable. But at that moment,
when I thought I'd broken both legs and electricity was shooting
through me, there was this blinding flash. The night filled up with
light. Later some guy standing on the corner said it was just the bus
changing wires but he was full of shit. This was a hundred times
brighter. Looking up from my knees, I knew. John Boy, I knew. Like
St. Peter on the road to Golgotha.

JOHN
What?

BRAD
Vision. I had a vision. Shining in the sky. And music, I heard music.
Cathedral music. You know what the vision, the message, was? . . .
This, it was this: The-Lawyer's-Duty-Is-To-Serve-The-Client. The-
Lawyer's-Duty-Is-To-Serve-The-Client! Swoosh! Suddenly I felt this
tremendous weight fall from my shoulders. Me still in the street,
knees bloody, trousers of my goddamn new suit blown out, the sky
filled with light and "Serve Thy Client" ringing in my head. . . .

Next day I deliver the closing argument of my life. The jury was out
long enough to get their free lunch and then they're back with a verdict that proved my vision in spades. I mean what's a vision without
a verdict, right? We-are-talking-a-monster-payoff, of which I person-

ally own 50% by virtue of my far-sighted contingency agreement. And the truncated client got rich too. Very happy ending.

I could hardly walk, of course. Had to wear a summer suit in freezing weather because of the smiles in the knees of the other one. But I was on my way. I'd received the wisdom I've lived by ever since. I call it the Golgothan Creed.

JOHN

You do?

BRAD

I do, I do. And now, John Boy, I want you to feel its strength too. I want to free you from your ignorance and stupid worries. I want to cleanse and empower you like a real attorney oughtta be empowered. So come around here and kneel down and repeat after me . . .

JOHN

Brad, I can't, I . . .

BRAD

You can! You can! Have faith, John Boy! Believe! Kneel down!

JOHN

What I'm trying to say . . .

BRAD

Believe! Come on around here! Kneel down and your world will change!

JOHN

I know, I know! That's what I'm trying to say: If I kneel down I'll break my cast.

BRAD

What? Oh yeah. Shit! Can't kneel on one and sort of stick the other out, huh? No? OK. I can lay on hands back there. Stay where you are. I'll come around the desk.

JOHN

No, Brad. Wait. Stay there. Listen, I think I've got it.

BRAD

Got what?

JOHN

The Creed. I've got it, I'm sure of it.

BRAD

Yeah?

JOHN

(Standing, hand over heart) Got it, with nothing more. Listen: My-job-is-to-serve-the-client, my-job-is-to-serve-the-client, my-job-is-to-serve-the-client.

BRAD

Well, that's it all right. But repeating the Creed while a veteran gives the touch is good. Know what I mean. Makes it permanent. Like a tattoo.

JOHN

The Golgothan Creed is tattooed on this humble associate, Brad, believe me. Big. Several colors of ink.

BRAD

Yeah? OK. Good. You understand the deepest part, the commitment. Think of it as religious. Well, sort of. Religion for a lawyer. A life of service, serving the client. Know what I mean. (Pause) So, you still want to do it? The minutes, I mean. I'm only trying to do you a favor.

JOHN

I'll go over the material right away, Brad.

BRAD

Good. That's great. That's my boy. Oh, yeah, one other thing. You'll notice in the notes, you were elected Assistant Secretary of the corporation, of McFarland Marine. Yeah, at one of the, unhh, meetings. I forgot to tell you.

JOHN

I was?

BRAD

Yeah. No remuneration but a great honor.

JOHN

I see.

BRAD

Hey, it is. Great honor. Gives you a special role. I'll make sure you meet Buster someday, lunch or something. Maybe even a ride on "Bubbles." The barge I mean, haw, haw. Doesn't matter, they look about the same. Haw, haw. But I forget, they sold the one that floats on water. Anyhow, now that you're a corporate officer, you can sign and attest to the minutes, after you get 'em done. Oh, and give my love to Ellen. She really looks terrific. It's wonderful. Amazing. Star athlete, gorgeous, . . . with you, a gimp. You are one lucky fucker. . . . On that front, anyhow. But watch out. She may be a looker but she's an even better worker. . . . By tomorrow morning at ten hundred. This could lead to very interesting things . . . but screw up, John Boy, and . . . (Drawing his finger across his throat, smiling.) I'll be back after lunch. See how the minutes are coming.

BRAD exits.

(JOHN sits quietly, then puts GIORGIO's cage on the table and takes GIORGIO out.)

JOHN

Hear that, Giorgio? Il Duce's got St. Peter on the road to Golgotha. A minor detail in that dude's pathology. (Pause) No meetings, but Brad says, "Where's the harm?" and Brad is our Managing Partner. . . . So why not save my ass, and possibly some of the weekend with Ellen, to say nothing of the future, and get with it. . . . Eh? What's that? "Safe for how long?" You think this might happen again? And besides, I'm doing something I shouldn't?

(Pause, then suddenly animated, standing)

Step right up, ladies and gentlemen! See John Boy perform the Impossible before your very eyes. Watch this amazing man, the Wonder Lawyer, sworn to uphold The Law and a stringent Code of Ethics, create an Immaculate Deception by performing the Miracle of the Great "As of." Hurry, hurry, hurry. Lift the flap and step inside as he prepares documents establishing as Absolute Fact not one, not two, but many events that never occurred. Let your scraggly-necked preachers whine about pearls and sows' ears, fishes and loaves. You are about to see The Real Thing, in the Real World. Pay your modest admission to see this brave man spurn prissy Qualm, tip-toe past Disbarment, and secure his future in the Everlasting, Deadly Jungle of The-Law-As-It-Is-But-Not-As-It's-Taught. Hold your breath as he invents minutes that never ticked. Oh, The Thrill and Where's the Harm? Hurry! Hurry! Hurry!

Lights down.

SCENE NINE

Friday, mid-day, JOHN's office. JOHN is feeding GIORGIO little pieces of cheese.

ELLEN enters, unseen by JOHN.

JOHN

Mangia, Giorgio, mangia. . . . Ahh, *bene, bene . . . Come sei bello, Ratto Mio.*

ELLEN

(Ambling toward his desk) What's going on back there, anyway?

JOHN

(Attempting to cover the cage) Nothing, nothing. Just messing around.

ELLEN

A rat! You've got a fucking white rat!

JOHN

Si, va bene, e Giorgio, il mio collego. Shares the office with me. Firm can't provide a private office for every associate.

ELLEN

Echh. I hate rats.

JOHN

But you're a lawyer.

ELLEN

Very funny. So are you.

JOHN

Giusto, carina. That's why I have *Ratto Mio*, here. I aim to explore the roots of our profession. My dedication is such that . . .

ELLEN

(*Interrupting*) Yeah, yeah, yeah. C'mon, what's with the rodent?
(*Moving away from* JOHN *and* GIORGIO)

JOHN

(*Petting* GIORGIO) Yesterday, on my way back after buying my
yogurt for lunch, I saw this kid with a baby buggy in an empty
doorway down the block. Maybe ten years old, had to be a truant.
The pram was covered with a dirty blanket. Had a sign, "Kittens for
Sale." You could hear faint mewing. When I stopped, the kid lifts
the blanket. There are five tiny kittens and off to one side, sitting
up on his haunches looking pissed, one white rat. "How much?" I
ask. "One dollah except for da tawtuss sell, dat's two." "For the rat?"
I say.

ELLEN

Why, for godssake?

JOHN

I don't know, seemed like the thing to do. I liked the way he carried
himself.

ELLEN

Jesus!

JOHN

The kid says, "No way. Da rat's da mutha, not fa sale." "Three dol-
lars for the rat," I say. Shakes his head, "Dat's a hum breaka. He's all
dey got . . ." "Hey," I say, revealing my stitches and tapping my cast
with my cane, "You gotta, I'm a victim." The kid rolls his eyes and
says, "OK bro, five dollas for the mutha." So I paid him, put *Giorgio*
in my pocket and came back. He spent the night here.

ELLEN

Where?

JOHN

Charlie loaned me one of his cages. One of his pigeon cages.

ELLEN

Rats, pigeons, cages for pigeons, pigeon cages for rats. Some law firm. Listen, about ratzo, there . . .

JOHN

Giorgio, please.

ELLEN

The ghastly animal, whatever you call it. If Brad sees it, hears about it, hears even a rumor about it, it'll be the end of your poetic, rodent-loving ass around here.

JOHN

Yeah?

ELLEN

Paranoid about such animals, totally.

JOHN

Incredibile! Il Duce, afraid . . . of rats?

ELLEN

Any of the order rodentia. Mice, rats, gophers, guinea pigs, gerbils . . . I've seen him leap on a chair at the sight of a mouse running under the bed.

JOHN

Bed?

ELLEN

Sofa, settee, anything, I dunno.

JOHN

No kidding? When'd you see that?

ELLEN

Oh, a long time ago, some firm party or something. Don't remember. Anyhow, be careful.

JOHN

Yeah, I'll keep him under wraps. . . . Look, Ellie, about tonight. Dinner's off. Least not till real late. Something's come up.

ELLEN

Right.

JOHN

'Right?'

ELLEN

Yeah, I'm sorry.

JOHN

You're sorry! I'm dying. Haven't seen you for weeks.

ELLEN

These things happen.

JOHN

Especially in this dump. (*Pause*) So, all dressed up and no place to go? Want to go on over to my place anyway? Don't know when I'll get home but . . .

ELLEN

(*Interrupting*) Oh, thanks, no, I . . . John, boy! You really don't look so hot. What's happened?

JOHN

"John Boy?" When'd you start calling me that? There's only one place you could've heard it.

ELLEN

"John," pause, "boy." An exclamation as in, "Whew! or "Wow!", or "Gosh! You look awful."

JOHN

Talking to Brad, huh?

ELLEN

He stuck his head in a while ago. So what?

JOHN

He should stick it up his . . .

ELLEN

Hey, he's the Managing Partner, my boss; I have to talk to . . .

JOHN

(*Interrupting*) So, what'd he say?

ELLEN

Oh, you know, a typical Brad remark, something about you spending the night with your jealous mistress.

JOHN

Right. You ask him why?

ELLEN

Well, he'd sort of warned me you'd be busy.

JOHN

Yeah? When did he do that?

ELLEN

Hey, you're really on my case. What's happening, John? Things like this come up all the time. You know that.

JOHN

They do, huh? Of course, you've been working here a lot longer than I have.

ELLEN

What's that supposed to mean? You know, you really are being a shit! (*Getting up and starting to leave*)

JOHN

(*Holding up his hand*) Maybe you're right, Ellie, maybe you're right.

I'm sorry. C'mon, sit down.

ELLEN

(Sitting, tentatively) So, tell me.

JOHN

He chewed me out and was getting ready to fire me, again.

ELLEN

What for?

JOHN

For not doing some work he gave to Charlie to give to me that Charlie never gave me, never told me about either.

ELLEN

Charlie? Why didn't Brad give it to you himself?

JOHN

Oh, he had his reasons all right. But Charlie's too smart for him. Too honest too. Anyhow, after I pledged allegiance to him, Brad decided to give me a chance to save my ass. A Friday late night all-or-nothing special. Something very important, vital in fact.

ELLEN

Well, that's good.

JOHN

For a very important client.

ELLEN

Doing what?

JOHN

I'm supposed to whip out some corporate minutes.

ELLEN

Oh.

JOHN

Phony corporate minutes.

ELLEN

I see.

JOHN

Doesn't surprise you? That's just good ole Brad, huh?

ELLEN

Yeah, well, sometimes you have to watch Brad. He gets a little intense. But why phony?

JOHN

You know, you're acting strangely.

ELLEN

Why?

JOHN

I haven't heard the old mantra.

ELLEN

Mantra! Me? Come off it.

JOHN

You know, "Cut, cut, cut!" We aren't supposed to ever discuss the firm, remember? Or our cases, clients, business. Your iron-clad rule.

ELLEN

Well . . . I'm just concerned. About you, that's all.

JOHN

I must really be in trouble.

ELLEN

Is this some of your paranoia, John?

JOHN

I'll say it again: There were no board of directors meetings. Brad's up-front about it.

ELLEN

I wish you hadn't told me that. I don't like it.

JOHN

Neither do I. Bald fabrication has become the price of a continuing salary . . . and, as he pointed out, of continuing to see you at work.

ELLEN

He didn't mention me.

JOHN

Oh yeah. Not only mentioned, he had a lot to say about you. Thinks you're a "powerhouse." You bring in "mondo moola." He also thinks you're a "dish."

ELLEN

What'd you say?

JOHN

About you're being a dish?

ELLEN

About there being no real board meetings?

JOHN

"Real?"

ELLEN

No board meetings.

JOHN

No board either.

ELLEN

What?

JOHN

Nope. Apparently what we have here is a corporation in name only.

ELLEN

No board of directors? There had to be.

JOHN

Once upon a time, around incorporation, no doubt. But something happened, directors vanished until there weren't enough even to constitute a board of directors. Just a couple of people, you dig?

ELLEN

Brad must have had some suggestion.

JOHN

Well, as for the minutes, he said just use "as of."

ELLEN

Huh?

JOHN

He meant I should write, "Minutes of the Board of Directors' Meeting as of . . ."

ELLEN

(Interrupting) The client's McFarland?

JOHN

Now, why'd you say that, Ellie? How'd you know who it is?

ELLEN

Dunno, just guessed.

JOHN

No kidding. I should take you out to the track.

ELLEN

I'm doing tax work on McFarland.

JOHN

For Brad, huh. Including the sub, McFarland Marine, by any chance?

ELLEN

(Nodding)

JOHN

Your 'big test', right?

ELLEN

When I got back from my, unnh, our long weekend, he brought me a whole lot of McFarland tax stuff. Most of it was routine. Then, I began to find funny things. One of them, sort of tucked away in it all, was this very big problem involving the sale of a barge. But I didn't have all the facts. When I asked Brad for them, he was rather vague.

JOHN

Basically, he asked you what would make it go away.

ELLEN

Unh huh.

JOHN

Ellie, we're at a crossroads.

ELLEN

Oh, God, don't get soppy on me now!

JOHN

And it's not over, either.

ELLEN

Much more of this and it will be.

JOHN

Yeah. The clock is ticking.

(JOHN *limps over to the sofa and begins clearing it off, tossing everything on the floor.*)

ELLEN
You and your clocks. That's what you said about sex too.

JOHN
(*Stretching out on the sofa*) Sad but true.

ELLEN
I notice it didn't stop you.

JOHN
Of course not. It doesn't stop anyone. Didn't you ever read Genesis?

ELLEN
(*A fatherly tone*) Look, John, I know it's hard. This is one of those things lawyers just have to work out for themselves. I don't know what to tell you. I wish I did but I don't.

JOHN
Have I asked you what I should do, Ellie?

ELLEN
You have to consider what you've been asked to do, and be careful not to assume things which may not be true.

JOHN
"A lawyer must never assume.". . . Of course, without assumptions life would be impossible.

ELLEN
And try to do the best thing for the client, for the firm . . .

JOHN
The firm, huh?

ELLEN
Always bearing in mind, of course, any possible conflicts . . .

JOHN

And the more it all bears on my mind, the more I take it personally. What he asks, it's not just wrong, it's insulting.

ELLEN

Or ethical problems. . . .

JOHN

And I've decided. I'm not doing his friggin minutes.

ELLEN

Your job.

JOHN

Yeah, especially now, with a rat to support. But I still can't do it. Why should I sell my soul to bail him out, I ask you?

ELLEN

Your future.

JOHN

My future lies not in lying for Brad.

ELLEN

As an associate in a prestigious law firm.

JOHN

Some law firm! If the Managing Partner had been earning his fees as General Counsel for McFarland, he'd have his minutes, honest minutes.

ELLEN

Yeah, but he has a lot on his mind. And maybe they told him they were holding meetings, doing everything right all along. Sometimes one does have to use little devices, phrases, "as of," and so forth. Just to tidy up, formalize things which were done informally.

JOHN

You think that's what happened here, Ellie? No directors, no board,

let alone no meetings is certainly "informal." Brad would like that
description. But I think it stinks. You hear what I' m saying, Ellie?

ELLEN

Of course, I hear you. At the same time, you have to realize I'm not
privy to the activities of the directors of McFarland Marine, John.
I really couldn't say what they've done or haven't done. But I can
say this, while Brad may sometimes be overly aggressive in a client's
interest, I don't think he's actively dishonest.

JOHN

As opposed to passively?

ELLEN

Nothing's passive about Brad. I've known him quite a while. I'm not
sure you realize . . .

JOHN

What?

ELLEN

Just how long.

JOHN

How long, Ellie?

ELLEN

Well, since college . . .

JOHN

Law school?

ELLEN

College. I had this work-study job in the law library. Brad was
teaching part-time at the law school for a quarter or something. I
used to deliver books to his office. In the course of my job. And we
got to know each other. Sometimes he'd give me a cup of coffee and
we'd talk about law, law school. I didn't know what I was going to
do after graduating and, of course, law school was a possibility. . . .

Pretty soon we're having lunch, then going out.

JOHN

(*Sitting up*) You and *Il Duce* were an item?!

ELLEN

Don't get excited. Nothing wrong with it. He certainly wasn't my first boyfriend. Whatta you take me for?

JOHN

Boyfriend!

ELLEN

Lover, whatever. And I wasn't his student or anything. Actually, to be completely honest, I scored him.

JOHN

You what?

ELLEN

Look, I hope this doesn't cause any structural damage but . . . well, women, girls, sometimes especially girls, don't necessarily wait to be asked to dance. And when the music stops, they don't necessarily feel they've been taken advantage of. Whatever they may say later.

JOHN

Is that so?

ELLEN

Don't want to get hooked by the hype.

JOHN

You? You went after Brad?

ELLEN

But I instantly lost interest and it's been over for years. I mention all this only to say that while he's somewhat pushy, well, I never found him to be . . .

JOHN

(*Interrupting*) You immediately lost interest. But then you just happened to work here as a summer intern.

ELLEN

That's years later. Besides, he'd helped me when I wanted to get into law school, he'd stayed in touch.

JOHN

Right. My point exactly. (*Lying back down*)

ELLEN

A woman's entitled to a summer job like any other law student.

JOHN

Anywhere she wants to work.

ELLEN

Anywhere she's offered work. Look, John, there's my job and there's my private life. I've done nothing to encourage him. Nothing. I'm super-careful about that. And I've always been very open with him about seeing you, long before we took our vacation together.

JOHN

I wondered where he'd found out. You tell him we were married too?

ELLEN

Of course not.

JOHN

He thought we were.

ELLEN

Well, maybe he just said it to see what you'd say.

JOHN

Yeah.

ELLEN

What did you say?

JOHN

I said we weren't, what'd you expect? I also said we weren't living together.

ELLEN

Yeah, good. . . Might as well get it straight. That's why I told him in the first place. Didn't want him to find out from someone else I was seeing you.

JOHN

No.

ELLEN

For your sake.

JOHN

Yes.

ELLEN

Didn't want him to take it out on you. Not that he'd stoop to that.

JOHN

No.

ELLEN

But he has strong feelings. Very competitive.

JOHN

And, 'All's fair in love and war.'

ELLEN

(*Pause*) I really ought to go. I've got to . . .

JOHN

Ellie?

ELLEN

Yes.

JOHN

When Brad told you he wanted to sack me before my probationary period is up, what did you say?

ELLEN

I asked him why he was telling me?

JOHN

And what did he say?

ELLEN

Actually, I overheard Maxine saying she'd heard Brad say that and then at lunch yesterday . . .

JOHN

(*Interrupting*) You had lunch with him, yesterday?

ELLEN

You knew that.

JOHN

I did not!

ELLEN

I told you!

JOHN

Like hell you did!

ELLEN

You asked why I was all dressed up and I said because I had a power lunch.

JOHN

And that's all you said.

ELLEN

Christ, John, don't be such a cry-baby! I have to see him. He's
the Managing Partner of the firm. He can determine my pay, who
makes partner and I want to make partner someday, the sooner
the better. What the hell do you think associates work so hard for?
What's the purpose of it all if it isn't to get ahead, become partner?

JOHN

Right. And after you make partner, well, there's always building your
practice to the sky, maybe a Justice Department job for a while, then
a bigger firm, a better offer, more money and so on unto the grave.

ELLEN

Right, that's exactly what it's all about.

JOHN

Life lived in the anteroom to life. Or, of course, we could end up
like Ernie.

ELLEN

Go ahead. Be bitter, have fun while you can. But Ernie's right on
point for you, come to think of it. Your days are numbered since you
cracked your gourd and smashed your leg. All of a sudden you're
more interested in fancy tricks with your cane and learning Italian
and playing with rats and hanging out with weird old men, than being a lawyer. You ridicule me and the law and then you turn around
and beg me and Brad and whoever for work. Well, fuck you! I am
ambitious! I do want to make it! And you are rapidly turning into
some kind of Retro Dropout! . . . I wish I knew what happened to
you, I really wish I did. You didn't use to talk this way.

JOHN

Neither did you, Ellie, neither did you.

ELLEN

Look, John, I'm no different than any other lawyer in this firm, male
or female, I have to see Brad. In the course of business. That's how
a law firm works! Sometimes I have to have lunch with the man.
Sometimes, like tonight, it's dinner uhh, . . .

JOHN

Dinner?

ELLEN

I warned you about that.

JOHN

Jesus! Yesterday you asked if we were still having dinner tonight.
And I said, yes.

ELLEN

You don't remember anything! Or you get it wrong! What the hell's
going on with you anyway? You don't remember me telling you
about lunch, and now you're trying to make me feel guilty about
having dinner with the firm's Managing Partner. You don't remember
a fucking thing, John Boy, not one fucking thing! You know why!
I'll tell you why: You're not serious anymore. You've morphed into
a dreamer, a nerd. Those cuts, the broken leg, aren't the half of it.
What's really happened, you've lost your balls!

JOHN

(*Silence, then calmly*) You're right about one thing, Ellie, I have
changed.

ELLEN

(*Long pause*) Johnny, I'm sorry, very sorry.

(*She goes over and sits on the edge of the sofa.*)

Stressed out, I guess. Don't guess, know. . . I'm sorry, honestly. . . .
Look, it'll be OK. We'll get through this. . . . (*Long silence, then quietly*) Remember? Remember the first time with this old flea house?
(*Patting the couch*) Working late, around two in the morning, I
went by your office, your proper, old office and you weren't there. I
followed the smell of pizza and found you up here going through old
files for Murray, listening to some rock station and eating this huge,
garish pizza with everything in the world on it.

JOHN

Marcello's best, *Pizza Mondiale.*

ELLEN

We'd gone out a little and I really liked you but you wouldn't make a move.

JOHN

Love, Ellie. I was paralyzed.

ELLEN

Amazing, considering how well you recovered. You gave me some pizza and opened a drawer and pulled out a bottle and two plastic cups. We had some wine and talked and stuff. Suddenly you got up and shut the door and stuck a chair under the knob. Then you went over to this sofa. God, I thought, he's got some grass or something stashed in that old walrus. You threw all the stuff on the floor like you did just now and you took my hand and we sat down. . . . And pretty soon the dust was coming out of this thing . . . I thought we'd suffocate.

JOHN

Still love your voice . . . and the trout stream.

ELLEN

We'll get through this.

JOHN

Sure.

ELLEN

You'll figure it out.

JOHN

I have, Ellie, I have.

ELLEN

Whatever you decide is OK with me. I mean that. . . . I'm just wired and, well, sometimes you really bug me. The fucking rat and above all, this learning Italian thing is the last straw.

JOHN

I realize Giorgio may seem sort of weird but my Italian? What've you got against Italy, Italians?

ELLEN

That's just it, nothing! I loved Italy. I loved Italians. I wanted to learn perfect Italian. Oh, Jesus, what I wanted to do!

JOHN

I didn't even know you'd been to Italy.

ELLEN

Yeah. After college. I came home full of so many new ideas, so many things I was going to learn, going to do.

JOHN

Ellie, learn Italian now.

ELLEN

(Shaking her head)

JOHN

Why not?

ELLEN

Law school finished off those fantasies. Like the incoming tide on summer afternoons. Castles, moats, labyrinths, turrets, nibbled away, collapsing, slipping out to sea. Entire civilizations, gone, vanished.

JOHN

That's very poetic, Ellie.

ELLEN

Yeah? Then I move to strike it.

JOHN

C'mon, you're sounding old.

ELLEN

I feel old. I feel like I've been on a highwire for years and years, riding a bicycle on a high wire and if I stop pedalling, it's the long drop. . . . Other times I feel like I'm suffocating. (*Long pause*) Well, I didn't mean to get into stuff like this. I'm just a lawyer now, doing what lawyers do. Jesus! What time is it? (*Jumping up*) I gotta go. Hey, I'm really sorry, Johnny, but I have to change. My duty dinner. We'll get together soon, I promise. We'll get through this.

JOHN

You mean change and pack, don't you Ellie?

ELLEN

Huh?

JOHN

For the country. You're having dinner with Brad and Brad's going to be in the country. You're going for the weekend, Ellie.

ELLEN

Well, yeah. So, what if I am?

JOHN

I dig you, Ellie, but sometimes you are really full of shit.

ELLEN

God, John, it's just more business.

JOHN

Flying blind. On auto-pilot man, sound asleep at the controls. (*He gets up and kisses her on the cheek.*) Go on, Ellie, it's OK . . . Go.

ELLEN *goes out.*

(JOHN *retrieves* GIORGIO *from his cage.*)

JOHN

Gone, *Ratto Mio*. My beautiful trout stream gone. . . . How I love her! . . . How glad I am to see her go! . . . She changes. Like the colors on the trout, like the surface of the stream, like the breeze coming down the valley, she changes according to her own secret currents, her own private weather. Her presence, her passion vanish into the ether, as she's lying there or drinking her tea or standing in the doorway. I never know what's real and what isn't. Is it what she's told me, or what she hasn't? Is it her warm, familiar gaze, or the dark glasses? Is it the angry message on my answering machine, or the calm, affectionate one she leaves a half-hour later as if she'd never left the first one? Does she even remember leaving the first one? . . . The same cycle, over and over. Joy, abandon, trust . . . faint tremors . . . then the break, *la rottura, Giorgio*. Next week, next month, she'll be back. Wandering in a another dream, beautiful, innocent, demanding to know what's wrong. With me. Tempting my poor heart . . . That's when I'll be counting on you, Ratty. Remind me, say, John, remember Marcel's warning: "What people have done to you before, they will do to you again. What people have done to you before, . . ." . . . Jesus, I sound like Charlie. He talks to his pigeon. I talk to my rat. . . Charlie! My God, Charlie!

Lights down.

SCENE TEN

JOHN's *office later Friday afternoon.*

JOHN *taps gently on the floor with the head of his cane. In a few moments footsteps are heard in the hall.*

CHARLIE *enters.*

CHARLIE
You called?

JOHN
I tap to apologize.

CHARLIE
Oh?

JOHN
I was an asshole this morning.

CHARLIE
Forget it, John.

JOHN
Hope you'll forgive me, Charlie.

CHARLIE
Things like that are part of being a lawyer these days. But apologies are rare and welcome.

JOHN
You were trying to protect me.

CHARLIE
Naw, more like trying to protect myself. Save my soul. Anyhow, glad you tapped. I had to come up for Ernie's stuff, have to secure the boxes. His sister called again. He's on his way here.

JOHN

Jesus! He's really coming?

CHARLIE

I told the security people in the lobby. They'll stop him. Gave 'em a photograph of the firm banquet five years ago with Ernie circled. He's staring across the room at the camera, looking miserable in his black-tie.

JOHN

What'll you do when he gets here?

CHARLIE

They'll call and I'll just take his stuff down to him.

JOHN

Brave man.

CHARLIE

What can happen with the guards there, I mean . . .

BRAD *enters.*

BRAD

How the minutes coming, John Boy? (*Silence*) What're you two creeps talking about anyhow? Shit, I can't trust anyone around this place. (*Walking around*) I spend half the afternoon at a power lunch while you two are up here in the ronin's roost playing pinochle or something. What the hell you cooking up, huh? Cabal of crips. (*Silence*) Boxes? What's in the boxes, Charlie? "Property of Ernie Tummel." Tummel? I thought we got rid of that dick. What're you still messing around with him for, Charlie? (*Opening one of the boxes*) Whatta we got here?

CHARLIE

Just the stuff from his desk, Brad. He never came for it.

BRAD

(*Pulling things from the box and dropping them on the table*) Izzatso?

(*Putting on* ERNIE's *hat*) Very nice, very nice. (*Looking at one of* JOHN's *boxes*) "Property of John Botz." Well, well. All of a sudden this isn't a law firm anymore, it's a goddamn storage business. What's your plunder, John Boy?

JOHN

(*Rising*) My things, Brad, from my old office.

BRAD

Go on, tell me about the minutes. While I look around. I can do two things at once. Hell, I can do ten things at once. (*Opening one of* JOHN's *boxes and pulling out a framed photograph*) What we have here? Unh oh, look-what-we-have-here, John Boy! The beach. Ellie in a bikini.

JOHN

(*Moving toward* BRAD *and pointing with his cane*) Put it down, Brad. Back in the box.

BRAD

No shit? "Put it down, Brad. Back in the box."

JOHN

That's right.

BRAD

Yeah, well, OK. Whatever you say, it's your hot pic. (*Dropping it carelessly into the box*) Let's get down to business then. The minutes. Let's see what you got done on the minutes.

JOHN

(*Silence*) No minutes.

BRAD

No minutes?

JOHN

Nope.

BRAD

Not done, huh? Well, that doesn't surprise me.

JOHN

Not started.

BRAD

What!

JOHN

I'm just following the famous Golgothan Creed, The-Lawyer's-Duty-Is-To-Serve-The-Client.

BRAD

Whatta ya mean?

JOHN

I've got a new client, me, John Botz.

BRAD

Man who's his own lawyer has a fool for a client, John Boy.

JOHN

And a lawyer who isn't his own man is the greater fool.

BRAD

Izzatso.

JOHN

I'm not doing your phony minutes, Brad. I quit.

BRAD

You're fuckin fired.

JOHN

Beat you to it, Brad.

BRAD

Like hell. I say you're fired.

CHARLIE

He quit, Brad. I heard him.

BRAD

(*To* CHARLIE) You stay outta this. Couldn't cut it, eh, John Boy?

JOHN

I think I got smart.

BRAD

Well, you're finished now. No more job. And no more Ellen, John Boy. You and your high ideals. Just an excuse. Fact is, you can't take the pace, wilt under the pressure, a goddamn wimp. Like Charlie there. Couple of stress wimps. (*Striding about*) And Ernie here. Let's not forget old Ernie. (*Tossing* ERNIE's *things on the table and floor*) Here's what your goddamn professional life will be from now on, John Boy, a bunch of shit in boxes. You'll never have a decent office again. After this, you'll be a fucking pariah. You'll wander from one stinking old building to another, renting one-room offices with frosted glass doors, trying to survive on whatever crawls in. You'll end up being a temp, scrounging for crumbs, contract work at sweatshop rates. Or maybe at a public service law firm where you can really learn about hypocrisy. . . . Look at this crap. Matches from the Chi Chi Bar. Old business cards, towel from the Restwell Motel. Mildewed snapshots.

ERNIE *enters wearing a long overcoat, unseen by* BRAD.

Property of a ghost, ghost. And that's what you'll be, John Boy, a fucking ghost, shadow creeping through the slums of the legal world. All that study and time and work and money gone to waste, turned to shit. Lost, you'll be lost with creeps like Tummel, squirming around in the dark on top of each other like maggots. (*Shuffling things in the box*) This is kind of fun. Like a rummage sale.

(BRAD *sees* ERNIE, *who pulls a shotgun from under his overcoat.*)

BRAD

Jesus! Ernie! Jesus!

ERNIE

I am not Jesus! I am not here to save you. I come to condemn you. I want you to go to hell where you belong and I am going to send you there.

BRAD

Just, just wait a minute, Ernie. Wait a minute . . .

ERNIE

(Interrupting) You knew she was crazy. Now you must receive your just desserts.

BRAD

Ernie, Ernie, now listen, please listen. I'm really sorry about that lady. I'd never have let you go but my partners made me. Ernie Boy . . .

ERNIE

Don't ever call me that again, you understand! Never!

BRAD

(Hands up) Yes. OK. Never. OK Easy. I understand. I'll call you anything you want.

ERNIE

Your Honor.

BRAD

What?

ERNIE

I said, your Honor. You call me, your Honor.

BRAD

Your Honor?

ERNIE

And Judge Tummel. Because that's what I am. I am your judge, Brad Thomas, come to render final judgment. You call me, Judge Tummel.

BRAD

Right, Judge Tummel it is. May it please the court, could we just recess a minute here without the shotgun and discuss, . . .

ERNIE

Denied! Hands up! Stay where you are! Did I tell you to move?

BRAD

Sorry. Sorry, Judge. Your Honor.

ERNIE

Now, just because I'm going to make a mess out of you, you don't have to leave my things in a mess. You're going to put everything back in the box.

BRAD

Sure, Judge, sure. (*Tossing things into the box*)

ERNIE

Hold it! Say, "There now."

BRAD

Huh?

ERNIE

"There now," like putting a child to bed, comforting a child. Can you do that?

BRAD

Yeah, yeah, sure. I can do it. Sure I can. (*Putting the matchbook in the box*) There now!

ERNIE

No! That isn't it at all. That's too harsh, too hurried. Slowly, gently, like you would your own child. Now try again.

BRAD

Listen, goddammit, I don't have any fucking kids anymore. Put down the . . .

ERNIE

(*Interrupting, thrusting the shotgun at* BRAD) You're in contempt of Court. If you ever swear at me again, I'll blow you away without any last words. Do as I said, now!

BRAD

(*Putting items in the box*) There. There.

ERNIE

Stop! Take those things out. (*Shaking,* BRAD *takes them out.*) Try to think: What'd I tell you to do?

BRAD

You said to put them in slowly . . . and . . .

ERNIE

And?

BRAD

And say, "There."

ERNIE

You're slipping, Brad.

BRAD

Please, Ernie, please. I tried to do it right. You said, you said to say, "There." Say it slowly, you said, with feeling, you said. Like I was putting a child to bed.

ERNIE

(*Pointing at* JOHN) What's your name?

JOHN

John.

ERNIE

John, tell him what I said to say.

JOHN

You said . . .

ERNIE

Tell him, not me.

JOHN

(*To BRAD*) He said to say, "There now."

ERNIE

Think you can do that?

BRAD

Yeah, sure, sure I can do that.

ERNIE

Is that how you address the Court?

BRAD

Yes, your Honor, I can say that, I can say, "There now," Judge.

ERNIE

THEN DO IT!

BRAD

(*Putting each item gingerly in the box*) There now. . . . There now. . .
There now . . . There now . . . There now . . . There now . . . That's
the last one, Err . . . Judge.

ERNIE

Is that your testimony, Defendant?

BRAD

Yes, it is your Honor. You can see for yourself, nothing left on the
table, nothing's on the floor.

ERNIE

Well, well. Seldom is it given the Court to witness a defendant demon-
strate the pattern of his deceit so clearly by his own behavior and words.

BRAD

Please, Ernie, I mean Judge Tummel. Look. Nothing's left.

ERNIE

You'd stake your life on it? You've put all my things back in the box?

BRAD

Yeah, sure, my life. Everything. . . . Your Honor. Judge.

ERNIE

Tell the prisoner what he forgot, Charlie. (CHARLIE *pats the top of his own head.*) I said TELL him, Charlie. What's the matter with everyone around here?

CHARLIE

(As BRAD *takes off the hat*) Yes. Yes, that's it, Brad. It's Ernie's hat.

ERNIE

Now, do your duty.

BRAD

There now.

ERNIE

More FEELING, man! . . . And gently, as though you mean it.

BRAD

Therrre noww, there . . . now. There . . .

ERNIE

That's enough. Sergeant at Arms! That's you, Charlie. Bring the prisoner over to the bench for sentencing and execution. Go on. (CHARLIE *leads* BRAD *in front of* ERNIE.) Good, yes. Stand there. Anything to say?

BRAD

What the fuck is this? Mother of God . . .

ERNIE

Silence. Now, kneel.

BRAD

What?

CHARLIE

(Moving between BRAD and ERNIE) Look, Ernie, I know how you feel, I been there . . . I've been there too . . . But this isn't going . . . Hurting Brad isn't going to help, it's . . .

ERNIE

"Hurting?" "Hurting Brad?" Charlie, believe me, he won't feel a thing. I'm going to blow a hole in him one of your pigeons could fly through. (Motioning with shotgun) Get the hell out of there, Charlie. Go on.

(CHARLIE moves away.)

Hurt him! That's rich. All right, Prisoner, come here and kneel. Right here!

(BRAD kneels.)

ELLEN enters and stands appalled.

(As ERNIE raises the shotgun, JOHN pushes the barrel up with his cane.)

(CHARLIE quickly takes the shotgun from ERNIE who drops his face in his hands and begins quietly sobbing.)

(BRAD makes a move toward ERNIE but JOHN places his cane at his throat.)

JOHN

Cool it, Brad.

CHARLIE
Do as John says, Brad. Go on.

(BRAD *backs off.*)

(CHARLIE *puts the shotgun on the table and takes* ERNIE's *arm.*)

CHARLIE *exits, leading* ERNIE *offstage.*

JOHN
Now, get out, Brad. Go on, leave.

BRAD
You'll regret this. You'll live to fucking regret this. (*Turning as he leaves*) I'll be back!

JOHN
(*Quietly*) You'll be back and I'll be gone.

BRAD *exits.*

JOHN
(*Checking the shotgun*) It's empty! I'll be damned. Wasn't loaded.

ELLEN
You were incredible!

JOHN
Thanks.

ELLEN
You were wonderful. You didn't know it wasn't loaded. And you handled Brad too.

JOHN
Didn't even think about it. (*Sitting down*) But now I'm scared.

ELLEN
My heart's pounding. I can't believe how brave you were.

JOHN

Knee jerk, just reflexes that's all. . . . See, all that fooling around with my cane paid off.

ELLEN

What the hell was Ernie trying to do?

JOHN

Just what he did, I guess, terrify Brad.

ELLEN

Well, among other things, this sure takes care of my weekend in the country, thank God.

JOHN

Yeah, Ellie, you post-modernized the old cliché about shotguns making honest women.

ELLEN

Very funny.

JOHN

Now that I think about it, what if I'd done nothing?

ELLEN

What do you mean?

JOHN

Eventually we'd all have realized . . . I mean how long could Ernie have stood there with an empty shotgun before we all got the picture?

ELLEN

Well, I like it how it was. And I'll never forget. (*Pause*) I don't suppose you'd still be interested in dinner tonight.

JOHN

Naw, but thanks.

ELLEN

Yeah.

JOHN

Ellie, . . . Thanks for asking.

ELLEN

Probably best. . . . (*Starting to leave*) We could be lawyerly about it, ambiguous. Call it a commemorative meal, to mark, you know, whatever. No fooling around.

JOHN

Yeah, I know. But not tonight. Some other night, maybe.

ELLEN

(*Kissing him*) Yeah. Maybe another other night.

ELLEN *exits.*

(JOHN *sits quietly for a few moments.*)

JOHN

Some sanctuary.

(*He stands, turns his hat around backwards and, putting* GIOR-GIO's *cage on his desk, takes him out and pets him.*)

Va bene, Giorgio? Ahhh, you're thinking you shouldda stood in the pram, huh? Thinking you've been adopted by a real loser. Well, listen kid, there's worse things than having a father who does contract work. And during the gaps, maybe we can get a life, travel a little, learn something new. . . . Anyhow, believe me, *Ratto Mio*, even if I never grow up, you'll like me a lot better than you'd have liked those kittens in a few weeks.

JOHN *puts* GIORGIO *back in his cage and covers it. He takes his backpack and cane and, turning to survey his office for a few moments, exits with* GIORGIO.

CHARLIE *enters as the lights begin to go down slowly.*

CHARLIE
Storm's over, Speedball. Time to fly. Remember: Home, straight home. Should only take you about an hour.

CHARLIE *and* SPEEDBALL *exit.*

Blackout.

THE END

JAMES WOOD, the author of *An Academic Question* and *Fanny*, practiced law in New York City and Los Angeles and served in a think tank, before returning to university to study playwriting and directing.